ABOUT THE AUTHOR

Charles S. Mueller knows teenagers and understands them well. He has spoken at numerous youth gatherings across the country during the last 10 years. His unique ministry to young people led him to write two popular books, *Thank God I'm a Teenager* and *Getting Along*. In these books he speaks to the questions most commonly asked by teens and offers comfort and direction to those searching for answers. *Bible Readings for Teenagers* promises to do the same for teens pursuing a stronger walk with God.

Early in his ministry Mueller served parishes in Silver Spring, Maryland; Jacksonville Beach, Florida; and at present is a pastor in Roselle, Illinois.

Bible Readings
FOR
TEENAGERS

Bible Readings
FOR
TEENAGERS

·

Charles S. Mueller

AUGSBURG Publishing House • Minneapolis

MANUFACTURED IN THE UNITED STATES OF AMERICA

*This book is dedicated to five great
Christian women, each of whom has helped
me in ministry as they have carried
out their own: Judy Kabat, Esther Kruse,
Audrey Mueller, Nelda Piper, and Judy White.*

PREFACE

Selecting the subjects for these devotional Bible studies for you teenagers was quite easy—I selected those that you said were important. To do this, I listened to the messages which thousands of you have been sending me for nearly 10 years. I have kept careful record of my conversations with young people. I watch for reactions (and for subjects that turn you on) among the 10 to 15 thousand of you I address each year at rallies from coast to coast. I read the questionnaires completed and the notes added in response to *Thank God I'm a Teenager* (Augsburg, 1976). I checked through the more than 5000 notes and scribblings that you have handed me, both solicited and unsolicited, at places all over the United States and some in Canada. A more complete sharing of these notes, together with specific evaluation and suggestions about what to do, can be found in *Getting Along* (Augsburg, 1980). In that book, you'll read more than 500 quotes of teenagers. I believe those written reactions reflect the attitudes and feelings of most Christian teenagers in North America. That's what made selecting the subject matter for these devotions easy. I listened to you kids.

The material in this book is organized in a kind of pattern. First are some general theological themes and foundational biblical concerns. Then the focus shifts to your interest areas—first to self, and then, very quickly, to family. The Bible studies deal with concerns at both those levels.

From family, the devotional subjects expand to friends and the place where most of you meet and interact with friends: school. A whole span of additional concerns in the areas of church, popularity, military service, money, careers, music, hobbies, and the like are presented.

It's time for the testing again. The devotions must be used by you to determine their worth. Only in your lives will their value be established. I offer this ministry to you in the name of our Lord, Jesus Christ. I thank all of you who trusted me enough to write, or who shared with me in so many different ways, or who made critical comments about yourselves and your worlds to me, or who helped unfold the wonder of life before my eyes. The beauty of what you did and the way you did it puts me in your debt for life. I hope you recognize your contribution in these materials, whether the offering was subject matter or insight!

And now, it's back to the pilgrimage and a continuation of the learning process. I might make further reports from time to time as I come to newer and fuller understandings, insights, and perceptions about you teenagers and the things you have committed to me to share. May God bless this service to you.

■ WHERE ARE YOU?

Gen. 3:1-10: "But the Lord God called out to the man, 'Where are you?' " (v. 9).

It wasn't that God couldn't find Adam! Not at all! He knew exactly where his one-time friend was hunched in the underbrush, hoping to be missed. God also knew all about that tragic moment when the prodding of Satan overwhelmed the shaky defenses of Eve, and when Eve's invitation to share in her sin captured the will of Adam. So his question didn't mean, "I can't find you!" It meant, "Now that you've decided to claim your destiny and throw off my loving directions, where do you find yourself?"

People talk a lot about captaining their own destinies. When they do, they want you to believe they have made a good choice in deciding to do things "their" way. Adam didn't find it so. The glamour he had expected and the wisdom Satan had promised didn't develop. Only shame surfaced—and fear.

Yet God was searching for him. He went searching to establish a new—although not a better—relationship. It would never be as good as it once was, but it would be better than what Adam expected and deserved. Why? God loved Adam. He loves you.

Thanks, Lord, for all the forgiveness I have received to more than cover all the failures I have experienced. Thanks for helping me see and accept myself with the eyes of your mercy and grace. Amen.

Have you ever "hid" from God? What made you try? Did it work?

■ WHO'S THE OWNER?

Exod. 19:3-6: "The whole earth is mine . . ." (v. 5).

The whole earth is mine. . . . " The arrogance of God. Doesn't he know the facts of life? To be the owner, you need a deed, or a certificate of ownership, or a title. You don't just go around saying, "The whole earth is mine"!

Maybe *you* don't, and maybe *I* don't, but *he* sure does. He doesn't even flinch. He sharpens those powerful words in another portion of Scripture when, through Paul, he says, "You do not belong to yourselves but to God; . . . so use your bodies for God's glory" (1 Cor. 6:19-20). Whether you accept the statement or not really makes no difference. God still makes the claim and demands the recognition.

That's not all bad though. He's not just an owner, but a *caring* owner. He's no absentee landlord who does nothing to maintain his properties! He decorates to please (think of a spring morning), maintains the place (think about the cycle of nature), and preserves everything with tenderness and intimacy (think about how he heals hurts and flaws in the world). The finest proof of caring ownership is his plan for your salvation, earned and fully offered in Jesus Christ.

Praise God, from whom all blessings flow;
Praise him, all creatures here below;
Praise him above, ye heavenly host;
Praise Father, Son, and Holy Ghost. Amen.

List three specific and personal blessings from God which you claim and celebrate.

■ SOME MORE ABOUT GOD AND ME

Gen. 1:26-31: "So God created human beings, making them to be like himself. He created them male and female" (v. 27).

People are more than animals who walk upright! Don't believe those who see us only as occupants of the highest rung on the ladder of evolution. That's a story folks invented when they decided to deny the existence of God and were still stuck with trying to explain how things happened. We didn't just happen. God made us. He *made* us.

That last idea might be tough to handle in school. But it's not tough to handle in the pages of Scripture. It's not tough to handle in the world of Christian experience. It's not tough to handle in the arena of faith. In Scripture we read again and again of a God who loved us so much (John 3:16) that he decided he would not only model us after himself (Gen. 1:27), but also make sure we were his children forever (Eph. 1:5). Whatever being created in the image of God finally and fully means, it ought clearly to tell us that we are very special to him. We are special not just because *we* would like it that way! We are special because from the first moment he called us to life, he intended that special relationship.

It takes a special God to stick with me day by day. I'm thankful that you are—and do. Amen.

Identify something in nature that makes you know God keeps caring.

■ TAKE YOUR CHOICE—
CHILD OR ADULT

1 Sam. 17:32-40: "How could you fight him? You're just a boy, and he has been a soldier all his life" (v. 33).

There is a difference. When you were a child, you really enjoyed dolls and cap guns, but there came a day when you no longer wanted anything to do with those toys. Now people no longer ask, "Whose little girl are you?" but rather say, "What an attractive young lady you are!" Those are signals that the move from being a child to becoming an adult is in process. Sometimes, however, the people around you don't recognize the change, and they get confused. That happened to David. First they argued that he was just a kid and couldn't fight Goliath, then they insisted he fight Goliath in armor too big for him.

Doesn't that sound familiar? Aren't you often caught between being "daddy's little girl" and "a-young-woman-your-age-ought-to-know-better-than-that"? Or confused by people who treat you like a kid and expect the judgment of a man—simultaneously?

What's the reason for this confusion? Could it be that we act differently at different times—sometimes grownup, sometimes like children? Could it be that we develop at different speeds on different levels? We thank God that even when we are inconsistent in our actions, he is constant in his caring and forgiveness through Jesus Christ.

 Help me recognize that being an adult is different from being a child, and help me forgive myself for failing to act the way I know I should. Amen.

What signals do you see in yourself that you are becoming more adult? Make a list.

■ CROSSING THE BORDER

Luke 2:41-52: "Jesus grew both in body and in wisdom, gaining favor with God and men" (v. 52).

There's only one story in the Bible about Jesus as an almost-teenager, but that's all we need. It tells it all. The story involves a family separation (that must have been frightening!), a family disagreement (that must have been painful!), a family communication failure (that must have been confusing!), and a family reconciliation (that must have been great!). Change the names, the specific incidents, the time, the location, and the event is a repeat of every parent-teenager misunderstanding there has ever been.

Life on the borderline between childhood and recognition as an adult is filled with the potential for feuding, fussing, and fighting. It's not an easy time for anyone—parents or teenagers. The way Jesus finally solved it was simple and direct. He went home, was obedient to his parents, and concentrated on four areas of growing up: 1) the intellectual; 2) the physical; 3) the spiritual; and 4) the social. The relationship between obedience and the other four areas is this: When you are calm in your relationship with mom and dad and listening to them, the other four areas are easier to handle. Maybe that's why God gave a Fourth Commandment.

Help me with the problems of living on the border between what I was and what I want to be. Let me listen well and learn quickly in every area of growing up. Amen.

Identify one improving change you have already made in each of the four areas of growth.

15

■ IN THE MEANWHILE

John 9:13-23: "That is why his parents said, 'He is old enough; ask him!' " (v. 23).

Aging is inevitable. Like it or not, you will physically grow each day and automatically take on some of the characteristics of the adult that is sealed inside you waiting to get out. Your figure changes. Your voice deepens. Your mind broadens. Your religious insight expands. But, like aging of wine or growth of a row of corn, it all takes time.

It must have been a remarkable day for that blind young man. Not only did he receive his sight, but his parents publicly stated he was of age—*grown up!* Was it because they were afraid to take a stand in a ticklish situation? Maybe. Whatever the reason, the result was the same: His folks said, "He is an adult." Except in very unhealthy families, that kind of approving admission will always surface. Its coming is usually too slow for the child and too quick for the parent, but it comes.

Now, in the meanwhile, have a romp. Enjoy each moment of this changing time. Each year will come at you in 365 day segments. Enjoy them. Get from them all you can. All you can properly take out is what God put in; what he wants you to have. Take it, but don't forget to say thanks!

Dear Lord, my grown-up time will come, I know. But thanks for this special growing-up time! Amen.

Take a look at your teenage life. What's about to get away from you untouched? Sports? Music? Boy/girl stuff? Classes? Family? Spot one thing and go get God's gift for you—before it's too late.

■ ARE YOU READY FOR HELP?

Matt. 8:23-27: "The disciples went to him and woke him up. 'Save us, Lord! We are about to die' " (v. 25).

It sure took them long enough to ask for help! These experienced fishermen—men of the seas—had to be scared witless before they turned to Jesus. They knew he could help. They didn't say, "Put on a lifejacket, Lord, we're all about to sink." They said, "Save us. We are about to die!" They *knew* he could help. By the time they turned to him, *only* he could help. It took a lot of fear for the fishermen to ask a carpenter for help at sea, but they did. And he gave it.

How's it going with you right now? Any fearful and unknown waves rolling in on your life? At home? At school? Among friends? Inside yourself? I'm sure there are, but I've got good news! He is as near to you as he was to those men in that boat! He makes a difference.

You do realize Christ is in your boat, don't you? He came aboard the day you were baptized (Rom. 6:3) and has weathered every storm since at your side. More than that, the waves answer to his command. Why be seasick in the tossing tempest of life? Ask for help from the one whom the winds and waves obey. He'll help. He'll help you.

 Lord, teach me to look for help—from you and from others you have placed in my life. Help me accept it too. Amen.

Where do you most need help right now? Write a prayer asking for specific aid. Be prepared for a surprising answer!

■ HELP YOURSELF

John 11:17-39: "Take the stone away!" Jesus ordered. Martha, the dead man's sister, answered, "There will be a bad smell, Lord. He has been buried four days!" (v. 39).

What she really meant was, "You can't do that!" Anyone who had the nerve to criticize Jesus with, "If you had been here . . ." was also capable of arguing with him in the face of his clear command. While Christ was preparing to do a wonderful thing, Martha wanted to argue about what was possible.

That same thing happens when people of any age are confronted, by Christ, with *new possibilities*. They are so involved with explaining what's wrong with their lives that they never get around to doing what he asks. They collect personal problems and catalog them, as if owning personal difficulties were better than resolving them. How sad!

Jesus once healed a man who was lame and then said, "Get up!" (John 5:8). How sad it would have been if the man had not gotten up! If he had been like Martha and said, "You can't do that!" all the blessing of the Lord would have been missed. But he arose at the command and claimed the healing. He walked.

Jesus wants to heal us of so many problems and give us so many blessings. He puts healing in your life and asks you to claim his gift. He says, "Help yourself." Will you?

 Lord Jesus, thank you for all the healings I have received. Help me recognize them and claim them. Amen.

Identify a "stone" that needs to be moved around in your life so that something good can happen to you. Move it at Christ's command.

■ GOD'S BETTER IDEA—THE FAMILY

Ps. 68:1-6: "He gives the lonely a home to dwell in" (v. 6).

Families are really something—they're so confusing! They help. They hinder. They encourage. They repress. They protect. They damage. They are great. They are a bore. They are all those opposite things at the same time. But, best of all, they are God's better idea. Just because we don't always know how to get that best out of a family doesn't mean it isn't there.

One super-special thing about families is that they give you a chance to make mistakes in a protected surrounding. When it's working right, the family is like a laboratory where all kinds of experimenting can take place—all in the hope of solving some of life's great mysteries. Mysteries like how to trust yourself, how to communicate deep feelings, how to forgive others, and how to figure out what chances to take. In a family, you can learn about love and care and truth close up. In a Christian family, you can see the human model (an imperfect reflection for sure) of the family of our Father in heaven and his Son, our brother.

God thought the family was needed and would be useful. Think about that, and about the fact that God established the family as his gift to you.

I'm not always sure the family is a better idea, Lord. I sometimes have tough times at home, but I have great times too. Help me to recognize the possibilities for the better. Amen.

Measured against "God's better idea," sit back and give your family a grade. How does it compare with others?

■ HONOR WHO?

Deut. 5:6-21: "Honor your father and your mother, as the Lord your God has commanded you, so that you may live long and that it may go well with you . . ." (v. 16 NIV).

The family *is* God's idea. Like everything in creation, it carries his divine seal of approval: " . . . it is good." But what makes it tick?

When you dig around in the machinery of family, looking for its power, the mainspring is a mother and a father. This mother/father unit is so important that God set aside one of his Ten Commandments to protect it. That is the only commandment that has a promise directly connected to it! Is there any better way of showing that moms and dads are special?

But what does *honor* mean? How do you do that? One of the understandings the word contains is that of weighing or measuring. When you "weigh" your parents, you are honoring them. But do a thorough job!

Sometimes, when we weigh (measure) our parents, we weigh only the bad things: They are judgmental, sometimes unfair, give more to our brothers or sisters, don't listen to us, can't understand our needs. That all may be true. But don't forget to weigh the rest as well: Their times of tenderness, their daily feeding, their efforts to teach, the words of encouragement, their efforts to understand. You must weigh it all! In that way, you honor. Be fair!

 Prayer thought: Determine the qualities in your parents that most bless your life and give thanks to God for these gifts to you.

Recognizing their humanity and yours, note on a piece of paper the two things your parents best do. Put the note where you will see it often.

■ LUBRICATED BY LOVE

1 Corinthians 13: "Meanwhile these three remain:
faith, hope, and love; and the greatest of these
is love" (v. 13).

A lubricant makes most things work better because it
cuts down the friction at the points of contact. Oil is a
lubricant. Powdered graphite is a lubricant. Love is
a lubricant.

Love is a lubricant? Correct! At the places in life
where misunderstandings build and tensions mount
and hurts fester and anger rumbles—at all those places,
love helps life function better, without explosion
after explosion. Love makes it possible to forgive, to
overlook, to understand, to let it pass. Love cuts
down harmful friction at the points of human contact!

But don't think love is blind—that it ignores reality.
For example, God knew exactly what he was doing
(and why it had to be done) when he sent his Son
into the world. Love showed him. Led by love, the
Son spoke words of judgment and condemnation.
However, he didn't stop there. He also spoke words of
peace and forgiveness! Love is what keeps things
smooth between God and us. When we practice love
in our own lives, things are smoother between us
and others too. The practice of love is especially
important between you and others who are in your
family. Let love lubricate your family life.

 Lord, there are friction points at home that
need to be lubricated by large quantities of
love. Let me bring the love that makes
forgiveness possible and life livable. Amen.

**Don't wait for a birthday. Declare a Family Love Day
now and do something special for every member
of the family. Surprise them.**

■ BROTHERS AND SISTERS

John 11:1-3: "The sisters sent Jesus a message: 'Lord, your dear friend is sick'" (v. 3).

The stories of Mary and Martha and Lazarus are among the loveliest stories in the Bible. Apart from the great resurrection of Lazarus, there is the tender washing of Jesus' feet and the "picky" incident when Martha wanted Jesus to make Mary help set the table rather than just sit around listening. We hear of the urgent way the two sisters asked Jesus to save their brother when he was sick. All that looks normal to me! Sometimes brothers and sisters fuss and fight, sometimes they love and care.

Aside from all that, what are brothers or sisters for? The easiest response I know is that brothers and sisters are for teaching and learning—both. They are for giving and getting—both. Brothers and sisters are to be bearers of assistance to one another. (As a matter of fact, if you say "bearers of assistance" real fast—and slur it a little—it sounds like "brothers and sisters.") They are to be all-around friends. See how it works? When brothers and sisters relate well to one another, each gives and each receives. That's the way God planned it. Brothers and sisters are special gifts to us from the Father in heaven.

Jesus, our brother, show us how to accept our brothers or sisters in ways that help us and please you. Amen.

Write a note to your sisters and brothers. Share with them at least one thing they have done for you that made you feel good.

■ YOU'RE OLDER, THAT'S WHY!

Exod. 2:1-10: "The baby's sister stood some distance away to see what would happen to him" (v. 4).

Every big brother or sister in the world has heard the explanation that explains nothing: "You're older, that's why!" It's the unreasonable answer to questions like: "Why can't Tommy mow the lawn?" or "Why doesn't Sarah set the table?" What it really means is that it's tough being older.

Big kids have to carry extra responsibility—that's the way life is. The older help the younger. They watch them, teach them, protect them. Unfortunately, they are often used by them, manipulated by them, even hurt by them. When that happens, it must be dealt with the same way that our Father in heaven deals with our abuses of his care toward us.

Having an older brother or sister isn't entirely a bed of roses either. The advantages should outweigh the disadvantages, but having an older brother or sister can mean occasionally being bullied, forced, or even shown a bad example. Yet when even that is put into the pot, along with being defended, helped, and carried, and stirred together, it tastes pretty good.

Having or being an older brother or sister is filled with possibilities for good and for blessings. Look for those possibilities.

You are the best model of an older brother, Lord. Show me how to pattern myself after you, so that whether I'm older or younger, I am at peace with others and myself. Amen.

Make a list of times your older brother or sister (or someone who acts that way for you) "bailed you out." How do you repay them?

■ SPOILED ROTTEN

Gen. 37:3-4: "Jacob loved Joseph more than all his other sons, because he had been born to him when he was old. He made a long robe with full sleeves for him" (v. 3).

If the chorus directed at some brothers and sisters is "You're older, that's why," the tag pinned on others is, "He (or she) is spoiled rotten!" That description is usually reserved for younger brothers or sisters who seem to be gaining advantages or achieving privileges which the older ones didn't have. It's sometimes true. Good parents know that fairness doesn't mean treating everyone alike; fairness means treating everyone with the same tenderness and care while recognizing that each person is different!

Remember too: conditions *do* change. Parents get older and often smarter. They realize past mistakes and try to correct them. Their financial condition may improve. They aren't as tense. All those new circumstances make for different choices, especially when it comes to rearing the second, third, or fourth child. A caring younger brother or sister is aware that an older brother or sister helped pave the way and avoids gloating over an improved circumstance.

Joseph was a younger son who found himself hated by his brothers for his father's affection. If something like that should happen in your family, bring the attitude of Christ (Phil. 2:5) to bear on the situation.

 Prayer thought: Isolate some areas of tension between you and the other sons or daughters of your family. Take them to the Lord in prayer.

What's your surefire way for getting your older brother or sister angry? For 24 hours, don't do that— or quit doing it altogether.

■ MY HOUSE SCHOOL

Luke 2:51: "So Jesus went back with them to Nazareth, where he was obedient to them. His mother treasured all these things in her heart" (v. 51).

Families serve many important functions. Right at the top of the list is this: they protect you. They protect you from real bumps and bruises, other types of abuse, acts of personal ignorance, problems too big to handle alone, and other frightful conditions.

Sometimes this protection is very direct—one or another member of the family will stand at your side and give the added measure of strength needed to confront a problem. Sometimes the protective device is more subtle. Instead of helping you face an enemy with force, a family teaches you how to avoid a confrontation or how to win with wisdom, wit, and words. The home is actually your first and most important school. It's an ideal protected place for teaching and learning. If the titles like son and daughter and mother and father and brother and sister weren't better choices, we could call all the others in our family "teacher," for teach we do! In the process, we learn how to handle ourselves in tense social circumstances, how to confront raw force, how to apply our minds to varieties of specific problems, how to render assistance when needed. With all that teaching and learning going on, there sure is a school in your house!

Jesus, you grew up in a home and learned much from parents and others. Teach me how to learn from those in my family, and help me teach others for the good of all. Amen.

What's the last thing someone taught you in your home? What's the last thing you taught someone else?

■ RULES TO GROW BY

Eph. 6:1-4: "Children, it is your Christian duty to obey your parents, for this is the right thing to do" (v. 1).

Ogden Nash wrote, "In the company of mules, there are no rules." Whatever picture that develops in your mind, his point is clear: rules are important. They help keep you from doing foolish things. They won't stop you, but where there are rules, you know when you've crossed over!

Having rules tells us when we are doing OK. If the rule is that you must be home by 11:00 P.M., you know that no one will yell at you if you walk through the door at 10:59 P.M.! Without a rule, you might have to guess how your parents would react.

Rules help keep us safe. Think about, "Cross with the light!" or "Don't swim by yourself!" or "Never wander around unfamiliar areas at night alone!" Lives are saved by rules!

Not all rules are that dramatic. Most just help life function better and keep us moving along lanes of love. Jesus learned rules. He learned them at home, from his parents, in an atmosphere that God conceived and provided: the family. Learning rules at home, with the family, is God's way to help you.

 Lord, I thank you for my home and for the rules I have learned that make living together easier and more pleasant. Keep me appreciative. Amen.

What's the most helpful rule in your home? Approve it out loud. (That means say so to your folks!)

■ IN OR OUT

Josh. 24:14-16: "As for my family and me, we will serve the Lord" (v. 15).

Certain things can set a family's boundaries, like your name, the place you live, or your style of life. Sometimes a father or mother will set a boundary by saying, "If you are going to live in this house, you have to live like we do." Boundaries establish who is in the family and who is not. Close-knit families have bold and clear boundaries. Loose-knit families have vague and casual boundaries.

What's the difference between these two styles? Why should we care about boundaries? Boundaries explain family responsibility. They help organize and order life. Boundaries specify who you can go to in time of need. They help you decide how to conduct yourself when you are faced with a problem. One of the surest signs of family health is a set of clearly established and willingly accepted family boundaries.

One way we determine important boundaries is by identifying those which God or God's people have already set and claiming them for ourselves. Joshua outlined a basic family boundary in the area of faith. He said, "As for my family and me, we will serve the Lord." Is that a boundary in your family?

Lord, people keep urging inferior boundaries on us. Help us to find your boundaries and live within them as your family. Amen.

List four family boundaries that improve the quality of your life. Can you also find two areas where your family needs boundaries?

■ NEW DEALS

Gen. 30:25-35: "Name your wages, and I will pay them" (v. 28).

A deal's a deal!—that's what some folks say. In a way they are right—once you agree to something, you ought to stick with it. Yet circumstances do change, so there has to be a way to review and change an old agreement.

Laban and Jacob had a deal. Jacob more than fulfilled his part under the old arrangement. But things changed over the years, and it was time to establish a new agreement. So they did. How? By *renegotiation.*

Renegotiation is an orderly process for changing old agreements—even those between you and your folks. Things like: How late can I stay out? How often can I drive the car? Just how easily those changes are renegotiated depends largely on you!

It will help if you adopt some rules for renegotiating. Be fair, make reasonable requests. Try to see it from "their" side and help them see it from yours. Keep your voice down. Lay off the tears and the temper tantrums. Don't get sullen or moody. Best of all, model your renegotiating after God's dealing with us. He "renegotiated" the old covenant and struck a new one with Christ as the key! In the end, you and I got what we needed, and he got what he always wanted: us.

 Help me change. Help me help others to change in ways that please you and help them bless me. Amen.

Where do you have the most renegotiating trouble? Are you too quick? Impatient? Demanding? Unclear? Pick out a basic flaw and improve it.

■ WHEN GOD SPEAKS

1 Sam. 3:1-10: "The Lord came and stood there, and called as he had before, 'Samuel! Samuel!' Samuel said, 'Speak; your servant is listening' " (v. 10).

God promises to hear when we send a message. Our messages to God are our prayers. But what do we call God's messages to us?

Some folks call his messages direct revelations. They say they actually hear him speak. Others say they receive written messages. Still others are reached by dreams. Those things have never happened to me, but I believe they could. I'm not sure they are necessary though. Why should God use an exceptional means for communicating when he has already used so many other forms? Like nature. Like his voice within me—my conscience. Like the Scriptures. Like the sacraments. These "messages" from God are clear enough and powerfully communicate his intent. He tells us that he cares for us. He shows us the extent and the beauty of his plan for us.

The clearest "word" of God is the Word-made-flesh, Jesus Christ, who by his life, death, resurrection, ascension, and present rule makes clear to us all God's love for us and his hopes on our behalf. We learn about Christ from the Bible.

When God cranks up to communicate, he sends a super message! Superclear too. Listen and learn!

Lord, I know you are sending the messages I need. Help me hear. Amen.

Spend five minutes a day this week listening using the divine communication device which best gets through to you. Then spend five more minutes with the one you have the most trouble understanding.

29

■ IT'S TOUGH TALKING WHEN NO ONE HEARS

1 Kings 12:12-16: "The king ignored the advice of the older men and spoke harshly to the people, as the younger men had advised" (vv. 13-14).

Talking with God is easy compared to talking with people. What makes it easy, by comparison, is that at least one-half the "conversation" is in the hands of a God who sends and receives messages accurately. People are more like King Rehoboam.

Rehoboam was a son of King Solomon. The people sent a message asking him to ease up a bit now that he was on the throne. They needed relief from taxes and other pressures of government. Rehoboam consulted two groups of advisors. One group heard the people's message perfectly; the other group twisted the message and made it mean something very different. Rehoboam listened to the message-twisters and refused to back down. The people revolted because the king could not (would not?) hear.

How about you? Do you hear? Do your parents hear? Brothers and sisters? Friends? Who hears? It's tough talking when there's no one who hears. Sometimes the problem is with them, sometimes it's with you. Sometimes they miss the message, sometimes you send a message that isn't easily understood. Be thankful that God sends us clear messages and also helps us hear them by his Spirit. How can you improve communication at home? At school? With friends?

Loosen my lips, Lord, that I might speak clearly; unplug my ears that I might hear. I need to understand; I need to be understood. Amen.

What messes up your messages? Anger? Silence? Pouting? Tears? Pick out someone and practice sending clear messages. Send one a day for a week.

■ CAN YOU BE TRUSTED?

Judg. 14:1-18: "Samson replied, 'If you hadn't been plowing with my cow, you wouldn't know the answer now' " (v. 18).

This woman from Timnah must have really been something. Either she was superslick and sly beyond words or Samson was easily fooled—probably both. She wheedled the secret of Samson's riddle from him and then told it to others. He found out, but too late. She betrayed his confidence. She couldn't be trusted.

How about you? Can you be trusted? Consider these three questions: 1) Do you keep your word and do what you promised to do? (For family members too?) 2) Would you feel safe relying on someone else in a tight situation who is as dependable as you are? 3) Do you go looking for chances to prove to yourself and others that you can maintain a confidence, keep your word, honor a commitment?

One of the earliest tasks of all real adults is learning to trust themselves in areas of dependability, confidences, and commitments. Keeping a secret is important, especially when someone else pays for it if you improperly reveal it! But trusting yourself and proving yourself trustworthy is important for more reasons than that. Until you have proven you are reliable, you haven't grown up.

 Stiffen my moral backbone, Lord, and help me to achieve trustworthiness. Help me for the sake of others as well as for my own sake. Amen.

In two columns, write out what acts of trust others can expect from you, then those which you expect from others.

■ MY SHARE

Luke 15:11-12:   "So the man divided his property between his two sons" (v. 12).

W ould you believe that one of the most common things family members fight with each other about when they get older is money? No, that's not quite right. Actually, they fight about *sharing* the money. The battles are over who got the most, or who should have gotten more, or who was cheated in the process. One of the most important things family members must learn is how to share. If they don't, everyone will eventually be hurt. Usually it's the smallest and weakest one who "bleeds" first and most. The food won't be distributed according to real need, or the shelter, or the clothes . . . or the love, or the care, or the forgiveness, or any of the other important things that make happy family living possible.

The fundamental force that makes sharing happen is love. God's written revelation, the Bible, tells us that in many places. Check out John 3:16, Psalm 103, and Philippians 2. How's the sharing in your home? Are you giving what you ought to give? Are you getting what you feel you need and deserve? Sharing with others helps them share too. Using the model of Jesus Christ and his caring ways toward us helps sharing happen!

Lord, you showed us sharing by giving yourself for us. We can't do that for you and don't have to. But teach us to share your bounty with others, beginning at home. Amen.

Write a will like your parents might prepare and "give" everything they own to others. *You* divide it up. How do your divisions show love?

■ LET ME CORRECT YOU

Luke 15:25-32: "The older brother was so angry that he would not go into the house; so his father came out and begged him to come in" (v. 28).

Some people say they don't mind being corrected. I do—I don't like it at all. I don't think other people like it that much either. Just look how they act! With the first word of admonition, they begin making excuses, or offering explanations, or disagreeing, or getting angry. No, folks don't like being corrected. But a wise person realizes that, painful as it is, being corrected is basic to learning. Two skills can help being corrected work better in your life.

First, practice *listening*. Don't warm up your excuse machine or heat up your resentment as the corrector speaks. Listen to what is said. No matter how it hurts, is the evaluation accurate? Does it contain the seed of something that could make your life better?

Second, *thank* the corrector. You don't have to say you liked being corrected. As a matter of fact, you can say you disliked it very much, but that you appreciated the person taking time to help you along. That approach loosens up the corrector who might just go on to say something like, "Well, I don't want you to think it was *all* bad," and then make some affirming comments you'd like to hear. It happens. Try it—at least twice.

 Lord, I don't like it when it looks like I'm not perfect. Help me conquer my pride and then more easily learn the important lessons of life. Amen.

Who's your best corrector? Who's the one with the clearest insight into you and your needs? Offer a prayer of thanks for that person.

■ IT'S NOT A ONE-WAY STREET

Luke 18:15-17: "Some people brought their babies
to Jesus for him to place his hands on them. The
disciples saw them and scolded them for doing
so . . ." (v. 15).

As Amos and Andy would put it, "Some days you
are the correct*ee* and some days you are the correct*or*."
There are days you are corrected and other days
when you correct.

Correcting is easier when you develop a few skills.
For starters, speak softly. Others don't hear you better
because you shout.

Use words that help the hearing. Pass up words
like *dummy, stupid, fool,* and any other words which
make you angry when used *at* you.

Package your corrections in a compliment. Nothing
is *all* bad. If you open your eyes wide enough and
look closely at what you are about to correct, you
will also see much that you can commend. Do that.
Correct *and* commend.

Stick to one main issue. Even though some other
less important corrections may also be appropriate,
don't make a lot of corrections at the same time. Stick
to the important one, or maybe two.

Be ready to admit it when you are wrong. Sometimes
the correction is incorrect. Admit a proven error with
as much grace as you can muster, thank the person,
and get on with living. That's how sanctified folk
function.

I'm glad you are never wrong, God. Make sure I
never think that way about myself. Help me
correct and be corrected. Amen.

**Make a list of words and sentences which help you
hear correction. Practice using them.**

■ HEY, LOOK! I'M CHANGING

1 Cor. 13:11-12: "When I was a child, my speech, feelings, and thinking were all those of a child; now that I am a man, I have no more use for childish ways" (v. 11).

Few things stay the same. Inevitably, sometimes almost imperceptibly, yet constantly, things change. In people, physical changes are most apparent ("My, how you've grown!"), but intellectual and emotional changes are just as real. All those relationships with parents and relatives, with friends and neighbors—they change too! One of the nicest things about this changing process is that it, too, was God's idea.

But there are also things which don't change. The need for divine forgiveness, the tragic reality of sin's consequences, the promise of God's daily care—those are just some of the things which don't change in life, thank God! That's right: Thank God! Thank him for the way life slowly but steadily and beautifully unfolds. Thank him for the supports that he sets in place in times of need. Thank him for providing "a way out" (1 Cor. 10:13) when the testing of life gets too heavy. Thank him for all the changes that make life better and the changeless things that keep life beautiful.

 You are changeless, Christ. While everything keeps changing around me, thank you that things stay the same between you and me. Knowing that, I can adjust to other changes. Amen.

Look into your closet. Shuffle through your dresser drawers. What evidences of change do you find? Put three evidences of change out in the open for a week as a reminder that you *do* change.

■ YOUR LARGER FAMILY

Psalm 103:15-18: "But for those who honor the Lord, his love lasts forever, and his goodness endures for all generations . . ." (v. 17).

Your family is much larger than you may at first imagine. In a real sense, it stretches back in time to include your older living relatives (and maybe a few dead ones, too—any famous folk in your past that you still proudly claim?). The sweep of family moves laterally, as well, to include aunts, uncles, and cousins. It then reaches a little forward to include nieces and nephews younger than you. The term *family* does not apply only to those people who live in your house! It includes more, many more! There's a name for those other people—they are called your *extended family*.

What's so important about your extended family? Plenty! In the extended family you learn lessons that are tough to teach at home. A cousin whom you trust (because you are blood relatives) will give you advice you wouldn't accept from anyone else. Your grandfather can be like a second dad, but he treats you a little differently because he has all the love and not quite all the responsibility of your real father. See how it works? That larger family eases the burdens of living and is part of God's blessing to you. And you are part of God's blessing to them!

As I look at my larger family down here, O Lord, keep reminding me of my much larger family that is gathering right now before your throne. Keep us in your grace that we may all be at your final family reunion, through faith in Jesus Christ. Amen.

Make a list of all your living relatives. Pray for them by name this next week.

■ POLITENESS AND OTHER NICE THINGS

Prov. 15:1: "A gentle answer quiets anger, but a harsh one stirs it up."

Some families feud, fuss, and fight constantly. I doubt if they know any better. Or, if they know better, they don't have the stuff it takes to cut it out. We might call them *evolutionary* families.

An evolutionary family is one which is left unattended and, as a result, deteriorates. Everything that is left unattended deteriorates. Unattended gardens soon overgrow with weeds. Unattended animals breed a scruffier lot with each passing generation. And families that aren't cared for steadily grow meaner and angrier and more unconcerned about each other. Striving toward the divine ideal calls for effort and concentration. But it's worth it! When family living is pleasant and attractive, when being at home is fun and makes good memories, it's no accident! It is the result of the practice of politeness (and other nice things).

Politeness? Come on now! Politeness? You better believe it! All those polite things that you were taught to say as a child and all those polite actions you learned actually help life. From politeness flows soft and pleasant words, gentle conversation, listening skills, caring acts, and fun. Try it.

Soften my words, O Lord, and stiffen my determination to say and do the right thing at the proper moment. May I mirror the tenderness of your care for me. Amen.

Organize a list of words and phrases that help others hear you. Practice ways to share the list with others. Practice on someone.

■ BRING YOUR FLOWERS NOW

John 12:1-8: "Then Mary took a whole pint of a very expensive perfume made of pure nard, poured it on Jesus' feet, and wiped them with her hair. The sweet smell of the perfume filled the whole house" (v. 3).

Funerals are great places to study family relationships. Some families find them a place for strengthening ties. For others, efforts to show genuine care and concern are abnormal and strained. Some will bring flowers or offer memorial gifts as a caring expression of their true feelings of grief. With others, expressions of grief and words of comfort are flat or stilted, inconsistent with their past pattern of concern. They may bring the flowers that custom requires, but their motivation is sometimes an effort to make up for past indifferences. As if that were possible! Death makes it too late.

It can be different. Bring the flowers now. Bring them to the living. Flowers brought to the living give you a chance to see their eyes brighten and their faces light up at the sight of your visible thoughtfulness and love. And they have a chance to smell *those* flowers.

You know, of course, that I'm not just talking about roses and marigolds, don't you? Bring other "flowers" too. Bring the indicators of love and care and sensitivity. Mow a lawn maybe. Clean your room for your mom. Help now. It beats bringing bouquets to a funeral. And it pays off here and now!

 Lord, Lord, help me make things more livable right now. Increase my level of sensitivity and stir me to express my caring. Amen.

Who in your house needs a sensitive act of love from you right now? Give it.

■ BEYOND FAMILY — FRIENDS

1 Sam. 18:1-5: "Saul and David finished their conversation. After that, Saul's son Jonathan was deeply attracted to David and came to love him as much as he loved himself" (v. 1).

Loving a brother or sister is great. But it's also possible to intimately care for folks who don't formally fit into your family. Ever heard the expression, "He loved him like a brother"? We address those we carry in our hearts with that kind of feeling by a special name—we call them *friends.*

If our family is our first "school" that teaches us much and protects us during the time of learning, the world of friends is our second school. Friends bring into the mix of life the experiences and thoughts which are beyond the sweep of our own family. Friends teach us things that we can't learn at home and, when we are far from family, our friends encourage and correct and support and guard us. Just like family!

Life without friends would surely be different. When Joseph Scriven wanted to write a line that showed the kind of relationship we have with Jesus (and he with us), he penned these words: "What a *friend* we have in Jesus." Isn't that a great and descriptive picture? That sentence helps us understand something very important about Jesus. It also helps us sense the fuller meaning of the word *friend.*

 Thank you, Jesus, for helping me understand by your actions what the word *friend* means. Help me be a friend to others. Amen.

Who's your best friend? Consider the qualities that made you pick that person. Do you reflect the same qualities?

■ FRIENDS BUILD UP EACH OTHER

Prov. 27:17: "People learn from one another, just as iron sharpens iron."

The Bible can sure say things clearly! Some of its teachings may confuse you and strike you as murky, but others jump right off the page. Like Prov. 27:17. Friends "sharpen" each other. That means they improve each other. They make each other better. They develop one another. Those are some of the things that friends do. The measure of the value of a friend (or a way to determine if he or she *is* a friend at all!) is whether you are a better person, a finer Christian, a more mature individual because of them. People who tear you down and make you ashamed of your actions aren't friends at all. They are your enemies!

How about you? Who do you lift up and encourage? What people get along better at home, or find school more exciting, or try to do something that expands their horizons in life *because you encouraged them?* Who did you help see a brighter side in a dark moment or an opportunity for growth hidden in what looked like a bad experience? What I mean is: to whom are you a friend?

 Lord, I hope none of my friends are duller because they know me. Help me sharpen them, and let them give me a keener edge too. Amen.

Pick just one friend and figure out how you can "sharpen" her or him in an area where help can and ought be offered.

■ FRIENDS REALLY HELP

Eccles. 4:9-10: "Two are better off than one,
because together they can work more effectively"
(v. 9).

Some folks have a faulty focus on friendship. They
see their friends as ornaments or prizes—things to help
them. It is true that friends can help you, but that's
really not coming at friendship from a very good
angle. A better approach is to recognize that having
a friend gives you an opportunity to help.

That's not all bad, you know. Helping others adds
a zest to life that many people miss. Great blessings
often boomerang on the helper. Even if the blessings
are not always obvious, it's important to know that
helping friends helps you.

For instance, helping friends gives purpose to life.
This is true whether others know you helped or not.
People who are philanthropists know that! That long
word means "one who loves people." Whether a
philanthropist gives 10 million dollars to a hospital or
changes a flat tire for someone in need, the effect is
the same. They have loved people. They have extended
friendship. They have helped.

Jesus helped. He helped when we didn't even know
we needed help or could be helped. Remember the
verse: ". . . it was while we were still sinners that
Christ died for us" (Rom. 5:8)? It's true. He was a
friend who helped, really helped.

 I'm not at all sure I want to lay down my life for
a friend, Jesus. I'm glad you did. Help me get
better at helping my friends, like you are. Amen.

**Be a philanthropist. Help a friend. Be specific. Do it
quietly and without notice. Afterwards, reflect on
how you feel about it.**

■ NOW THE BAD NEWS

Mark 14:43-50: "Then all the disciples left him and ran away" (v. 50).

Sooner or later you will discover some real bad news about friends. So, how about now? Ready? Not only do friends need help, not only is helping a friend crucial to maintaining a friendship, but (and here comes the bad news) friends can fail you. They can really let you down. At a time when you desperately need a friend to stand by your side and help you across a difficult moment, a friend might just let you down. Worse yet, your friend might be the one who caused the problem! It happens.

Jesus experienced that. All his friends bailed out when the pressure built. But he didn't leave them. Jesus not only *had* friends (who failed) but he *was* a friend (who never failed). *Friending* is a two-way street. When someone else goofs up that doesn't mean you have the right to do the same thing. No, when friends fail, that only sets the stage for doing something really friendly: forgiving.

I didn't say for*getting*. I said for*giving*. Forgiving means three things in the Bible: 1) send away, 2) let go, and 3) cover over. When friends fail (or when you fail a friend), it's time to think about forgiveness. It's time to ask for it or offer it or accept it—it all depends on who failed. Forgiving turns bad news into good news.

Lord, I need a forgiving disposition. Only you can give me that. Allow me that blessing, for my sake—and for the sake of my friend. Amen.

1) Forgive a friend who failed you; 2) Forgive yourself for failing a friend.

■ OLDIES BUT GOODIES

Ruth 1:1-18: "But Ruth answered, 'Don't ask me to leave you! Let me go with you. Wherever you go, I will go; wherever you live, I will live. Your people will be my people, and your God will be my God' " (v. 16).

Sometime in Ruth's relationship to Naomi, she got to be a lot more than just a daughter-in-law to her mother-in-law. Ruth and Naomi liked and respected one another. They became good friends. From the seed of their friendship developed another of the branches on the tree of Jesse from which bloomed the rose, Jesus Christ. That's what can happen when a younger person seeks out, develops, and claims a friendship with someone older.

An older friend? Why not? Why not look for someone older who has your ideals and goals and understandings, and then see if a friendship can grow? It happens all the time. Teachers, coaches, pastors, employers, policemen, aunts, next-door neighbors have all become lifelong friends to younger people in the past. Older friends bring a perspective that can take the sting out of some of life's tough situations and can ease the learning process in others. Ruth's relationship with Naomi brought some great things later in the lives of both of them.

See if there isn't some older person around you with that potential for friendship. Develop the potential. Do it for their sake—and yours.

Heavenly Father, I'm sure glad you are an older friend to me. I know you are because there is no one older than you, and you help me regularly and with such understanding. Amen.

Do something nice for one of your older friends.

43

■ A NERVOUS FACT ABOUT FRIENDSHIPS

Prov. 18:24: "Some friendships do not last, but some friends are more loyal than brothers."

After more than 25 years in the ministry, I've learned a lot about people—how they act and how they relate to one another. One of the fascinating things I've noticed about life is that no one gets into trouble by themselves. When problems develop, you can always ask, "Who was with you?" and out will pop someone's name. As an interesting reverse, whenever I hear of a parishioner in trouble, I'm pretty good at guessing who else was there.

Friends have a way of shaping the time you spend with them. Some build up people and events; others tear down. Some cause things to get better; others make things worse. Some people challenge you to grow; others sap your strength. You can't pick your parents or your relatives, but you sure can pick your friends. One of the consistent messages of the book of Proverbs is just that: Pick your friends. Just as important, the writer tells us that when you've gained a good friend, treat her (or him) as a costly treasure, for they are more precious than gold. And you know what gold is worth today!

Bless me with understanding, Lord, that I can recognize those who will be good friends. Help me keep the best. Help me change the rest. Amen.

Decide to read one chapter of the book of Proverbs each day. Underline the verses about friends. You'll be done in a month.

■ UNDER PRESSURE

Mal. 3:16-18: "Then the people who feared the Lord spoke to one another and the Lord listened and heard what they said" (v. 16).

You are under pressure from others your age; we call it *peer pressure*. Look around. Notice all the similarities you see among the kids your age at your school—their clothes, the way they talk, their hairstyles, music, values.

Many parents fear peer pressure. They worry it may destroy young people's values, or change their personalities, or lead them to drink and drugs. We'll share a little about that part tomorrow, but right now let's focus on the understanding that peer pressure can be pressure *to do good.*

Good friends really watch and watch out for each other. Good friends don't just stand around and let a pal go to pot or watch as someone they care about turns into a tramp. Good friends start putting on the pressure. They use words and offer cautions. They make comments and give advice. They set an example and repeat friendly warnings. If the problem is severe enough, they even make threats and are ready to use physical force. Good friends are just as actively interested in helping as others are in hurting.

When you see a friend in need, help out: put on some positive peer pressure.

Lord, I thank you that you came to me in my need. Your Son saved me. Your sent Spirit called me to faith. What a friend you are. Help me reflect that kind of friendship to my friends.

Decide to give some good advice to a friend today. Apply a little positive pressure. Choose your comments carefully and offer them sensitively.

■ UNDER SINFUL PRESSURE

Prov. 1:10-19: "Son, when sinners tempt you, don't give in" (v. 10).

There are at least two things happening while someone is tempting you to do wrong. First, you are being tempted. Someone is putting negative pressure on you to do what you know is wrong. Second, you are deciding on your response. You can either consent and become part of the sin, or you can resist and perhaps rescue not only yourself, but the temptor as well. Keep the two activities separate. The one is something the temptor is doing; the other is your role.

No one "falls" into sin as if it were an accident. There is always a moment (be it ever so brief) when a vigorous no can still win the day. If there is no such response, it's because you decided not to give it. You decided to go along with the temptation. Don't dress up the event in finer clothes than it deserves. It's the same old calculated rebellion that has torn up lives since the Garden of Eden.

Sin *will* come knocking at your door, sometimes brought by someone you claim as a friend. Learn to recognize it. (Here's a place where an older friend can help!) Resist it in the name of Jesus Christ. When others do their thing (tempt), you do your thing (resist).

 You struggled with sin, Lord, and overcame. Help me do the same. And when I falter, please forgive. I know you will. Amen.

What's tempting you today? Plan how to say no, and then say it.

■ A RISK OF FRIENDSHIP

Job 19:13-22:   "My closest friends look at me with disgust; those I loved most have turned against me" (v. 19).

There is a great old song entitled, "You Always Hurt the One You Love." I'm not sure that's absolutely true, but if you turn the title around a bit, one of the risks of any friendship surfaces. Try reading the title this way: "Only those you love can really hurt you." That's closer to the truth.

To accept someone as a friend is to risk being hurt. You have expectations which they will not realize. You have feelings which they will abuse, be it ever so unintentional. You offer aid and advice which they will blithely ignore. Sometimes, at your point of deepest need, you cry out and they will not respond. All that hurts. It hurts because you expected so much more from them than they produced.

You've got a friend who knows all about that. At the critical moments of his life, he was abandoned too. Friends slept through his crises. They argued through his times of inner struggle. They misunderstood his intentions. But he loved them. He met their acts of ignorance (and intent) with forgiveness.

Take the risk of friendship. Prepare for the pain. Keep forgiveness at hand.

 Let me see the flaws of my friends, O Lord, and help me keep on loving them anyway, like you did. Don't let me be hurt. Amen.

Remember a time that a friend let you down. Write out what happened. Burn what you wrote as an act of forgiveness.

■ ON BEING A THING

Gen. 21:9-11: "Sarah saw them and said to Abraham, 'Send this slave girl and her son away. The son of this woman must not get any part of your wealth' " (v. 10).

The story of Sarah and Hagar and Abraham is a sordid recitation of impatience, insensitivity, and disobedience. It's just loaded with sin. It ends up with Sarah insisting that Abraham abandon Hagar and her son (and his), Ishmael. Tragedies like that are possible only if someone totally depersonalizes another person and turns them into a "thing." Things don't have feelings (you think). Things can take any treatment (you think). Things don't need love and understanding (you think). Things are there to satisfy your needs (you think).

The quickest way to have those crazy attitudes chased away is to have someone try to turn you into a thing. How? When someone takes you to a dance because they need a date (but doesn't particularly like you), or when people start talking about "teenagers" (whoever they are) or "farm kids" (what's that?), they are turning you into a thing. Don't turn other people into things. Don't let them turn you into a thing either!

 I'm glad you know me by name, dear Lord, and understand my individual needs as well. Help me to reflect your kind of intimate caring in my attention to others. Amen.

Think about some titles that can turn people into things. How about these: mother, father, teacher. How can you keep reminding yourself that all those titles are people?

■ ONE FINAL FACT ABOUT TRUE FRIENDS

Prov. 27:6: "A friend means well, even when he hurts you. But when an enemy puts his arm around your shoulder—watch out!"

People who count can say things that hurt. They don't intend to; they are usually only being honest. They might mask their honesty with a little laugh or some softer words, but it pains anyway! Yet the only reason they say anything at all is because they are your friends. One translation of the Bible reference for today calls those kinds of corrections by a friend "faithful wounds."

You wouldn't want it any different, would you? Would you want a friend to conceal things you need to know about yourself, like how you come across to others, and why? Would you want a friend to fool you into thinking things were different between you and another special person than they really are? Of course not. You want a friend to be honest and truthful no matter what. But it still hurts.

Think about that when you must speak a correction to a friend. Make your message as gentle and bearable as you can. Tenderize your comments. Wrap them in love. Place them gently into the conversation. Be kind. Maybe the best way to describe what you ought to do is this: Be a *real* friend.

 How gently you correct me, Lord. You know my feelings can only take so much. Thanks for realizing that. Help me toughen my tenderness and tenderize my toughness toward others. Amen.

Thank (or do a thankful thing) for an honest friend who unintentionally hurt you while trying to help you.

■ FRIENDS OF ANOTHER GENDER

Gen. 2:18-25: "He formed a woman out of the rib and brought her to him" (v. 22).

It's going to happen to you someday (maybe already?). It's really going to happen! You are going to discover that you can have *friends of the other gender.* You will discover you can have friends who are boys *and* friends who are girls—both kinds. As a matter of fact, you'll discover that friends of the sex opposite yours bring a dimension to life you didn't realize was available. It's not that you've been dumb, you simply haven't been ready. Those discoveries are like time-release pills. They explode in a pattern, from time to time, as you grow older and more mature.

One of the nicest things about the other sex is that not only do they noticeably improve the quality of your life, they are actually God's idea. Knowing that helps you develop a useful relationship with them. As God's idea they are not put here for abuse or insensitive use or to be just a "thing." Whether you ever marry or not, that other kind of human being was put into the world, and into your life, to help you combat loneliness and unwanted aloneness.

Thank God for men and women, male and female—potential friends of another gender.

 All your good gifts brighten life, Lord. Thanks for friends who are boys and friends who are girls. What a nice selection. Amen.

Reflect on when you first discovered you can have friends of the other sex. Do you recall the person who helped you know that? Say a thank you to God for that specific person.

■ OOPS! I THINK I'M IN LOVE

Gen. 29:5-20: ''Jacob was in love with Rachel, so he said, 'I will work seven years for you, if you will let me marry Rachel' '' (v. 18).

The story of Jacob and Laban and Leah and Rachel is the stuff soap operas are made of. Not all you read about those people is a great recitation of faith! Their actions also add up to a story of deceit and moral weakness and bickering and marital uncertainty. But when it all started, Jacob was in love.

Love is the word we use to describe the shift you make from having a friend who is boy (or girl) to having a boyfriend (or girlfriend). It's an extension of friendship. It's an intense emotion toward which many healthy relationships naturally progress.

One of the most interesting things about love is that it is never defined. Not in the Bible. Not in the dictionary. What passes for a definition actually is a description of how love acts. Test that out by reading over the great love chapter of the Bible, 1 Corinthians 13. Doesn't it describe love rather than define it?

Love is great. It can be like a powerful friendship. It's not surprising that it often sprouts and develops in the seedbed of healthy affection and after a time of fun with one of those "opposite genders." Enjoy it. It's another gift for you from the Creator who not only thought up male and female but invented, and then first practiced, love.

Thanks for love, Lord. It's great you sent it. It's great getting it. It's just great, and so are you. Amen.

Describe how love looks to you. Write it down. Review and improve on your description from time to time!

■ SOME SPELL IT S-E-X, OTHERS SPELL IT S-I-N

2 Sam. 13:1-15: "I'm in love with Tamar, the sister of my half brother Absalom" (v. 4).

Some people think the synonym for love is sex. It's not. Sexual relations are a wonderful and patterned part of God's intention for men and women—in marriage. Sexual relations become the seal of a commitment to publicly establish and keep improving a life of love between one man and one woman until death makes that impossible. That's not some old-fashioned ideal, it's God's clear intent.

When sexual urgings dominate a boy-girl relationship, love has a hard time developing. Sexual urgings without a practiced commitment wear away at true love because someone is being used. A regular final result of sexuality outside the boundary of a public, practiced commitment is described in 2 Samuel 13: ". . . he hated her now even more than he had loved her before" (v. 15). Sex outside of marriage is spelled s-i-n. Whenever sin romps across our lives something dies. It could be love. Or respect. Or a godly relationship. Or you. Don't spell s-e-x as s-i-n.

I'm glad you made me sexual, God. That opens doors to new and exciting experiences. Help me honor you and bring a blessing to others in the way I use this gift.

In the world of sexuality, *love* and *lust* look a lot alike. But one is from God and the other from Satan. Develop a test to discriminate between the two.

■ WHO'S GOING TO TELL ME ABOUT SEX?

Gen. 4:1: "And Adam knew Eve, his wife . . ." (KJV).

I'll bet I read Genesis 4:1 a hundred times before I realized that "knew" meant Adam and Eve had sexual relations. Once I understood that I began discovering that the Bible is chock full of good advice and important comments about sex and sexual relations. But no one told me; I found out by myself.

I strongly believe teenagers have a right to ask questions about sex, and they've got a right to receive clear answers. If everything else is balanced, one of the best places to hear about sex is in your own home, from your mom and dad. But not all moms and dads are equally gifted in explanations (you'll also discover that some moms and dads don't know the answers themselves), so be prepared to look for help in other places. Then you can tell your folks what you've learned, and together you can share new understandings.

Where can you look for advice about sexual matters? Ask your doctor. Ask your pastor. Ask your school counselor. Wherever you turn, test out what you are told against the Word of God, the Scriptures. Good advice reinforced by the "good book" is a combination that's hard to beat.

There are times, Lord, that I need to know more than I understand. Lead me to someone who won't mislead. In Jesus' name.

Get a good book on human sexuality. Read it. Talk it over with someone you trust.

■ READY, ABLE, BUT UNWILLING

Gen. 39:2-20: "How then could I do such an immoral thing and sin against God?" (v. 9).

A lot of people would say that Joseph was stupid, or that he got a bad deal, or was too scared to take advantage of his big chance to *really* live! None of those things is true. He was a moral child of God who believed that no was the right answer when tempted to sin.

There are times in life you will have to say no. Temptations, testings, and trials will come. They'll come in more areas than just sexuality! Your honesty, your trustworthiness, your dependability, your very integrity will all be tested. But your earliest real powerful test will probably come in the area of your sexuality. Why? Because you are sexually ready and able long before you are prepared to enter into the kind of lifelong relationship God has in mind for you. Maybe the reason we are ready so early is that our readiness prepares us to practice saying no to things which are pretty straightforward. Later in life temptations get trickier!

Sexual urgings can be controlled a number of ways. The best is by staying away from situations which sexually stimulate you—certain movies, people, places, conversations. Learn how to "no" what's wrong so that you can be ready to eagerly "yes" what's right.

 Am I as weak and wishy-washy as I think, Lord? *Spirit*-ualize me, for I need it. Help me avoid temptation too. Amen.

Identify three things to which you should say no when tested. Add to your list.

■ KEEP COOL, BUT DON'T FREEZE

Gen. 1:27-28: "[God] blessed them, and said, 'Have many children, so that your descendants will live all over the earth and bring it under their control'" (v. 28).

Don't get God wrong. He believes in sex. He just doesn't believe in the kind of sex that ends up with someone getting hurt. That's the inevitable result for those who use sex wrong. Those who say that's not so are like the punch-drunk fighter who claims blows to the head don't do damage—at least not to him. Some folks are so sexually punch-drunk God has turned them over to their excesses (Rom. 1:26-32).

But we're not going to give this good gift of God to the world and close it off to Christians! No way. We claim it. Rejoice in the many facets of your sexuality. One good way to do that is by remembering the advice on the mayonnaise jar: "Keep cool, but don't freeze."

Will every loving contact lead in a beeline to sexual excess and abuse? Not if you don't want it to. If you know how to keep your cool (and help your partner do the same) there are a lot of exciting areas to be experienced and explored. But be straightforward with your partner on the adventure and careful that you don't put a larger burden on him (or her) than he (or she) can handle. Look out for yourself too! Then have fun—lots of it.

Let me be a good date, Lord. Let me be good for my date, Lord. Let my date be good to me. Amen.

Start a list of those qualities that you would like in your mate for life. Who do you know that might match your expectations?

55

■ BESIDES, I'VE GOT SCHOOL TOMORROW

Luke 2:52: "Jesus grew both in body and wisdom, gaining favor with God and men."

During the teens tons of important things are happening. Each day you learn how to handle new experiences. Everywhere you turn someone is trying to teach you something new. Not only is your home a "school" (remember that?), but practically every other place is a "school" as well. While recognizing the universal character of your educational process (how's that for a heavy sentence!), don't forget the obvious: School is for school too.

That's right. School is for school. Your school is an important place to learn a lot of things in a systematic fashion. Some of the things you'll like learning the moment you try. Other subjects will make you almost gag. Some things will be easy. Others, even though you enjoy working at them, will be tough to get straight. Your most important task in school is not *learning* new information; it's learning *how to learn* new information. Once you get that down you are ready for an education! So keep it in focus: sex isn't the only subject you need to know more about; it's just one of many. School is where you get your chance to learn about a lot of things, all of them important.

Lord, let me see what I'm missing when I don't see what I'm missing at school. Amen.

Let's get some system into your selection of a lifetime career. Make a list of the careers you find interesting enough to want to know more about.

■ GROWING UP IN SCHOOL: LESSON ONE

Mark 12:28-31: "The second most important commandment is this: 'Love your neighbor as you love yourself' " (v. 31).

Right up at the top of the list of things I need to learn at school is this: I'm in charge of me—and I better take care of myself!

Reread the scripture text above, then answer this: "Can you love someone else if you don't love yourself?" If Jesus tells you to love others as you love yourself, what happens if you don't have any real concern for you? The answer is obvious—you won't care about others either!

Imagine that you are coming to yourself, as a friend, for some advice. Try these questions on for size. Give yourself the best answers you can.

1. What can I do to make my feelings about school more positive?
2. What's wrong with the kind of friends I have?
3. What do I have to do to be liked more?
4. Why am I sometimes restless and unsettled?

Answer them for yourself. Be serious. Do a good job. In the answering this fact will become even more evident: You are in charge of you. Be a good friend to yourself. That's one part of becoming a good friend to others.

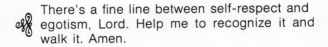 There's a fine line between self-respect and egotism, Lord. Help me to recognize it and walk it. Amen.

**Decide to do something that you have wanted to do but haven't been able to get started. Do it.
You're in charge of you.**

■ GROWING UP IN SCHOOL: LESSON TWO

Gen. 25:24-28: "The boys grew up, and Esau became a skilled hunter, a man who loved the outdoors, but Jacob was a quiet man who stayed at home" (v. 27).

Assuming that peer pressure is real (and it is), and assuming that young people don't like to be out of step (and they don't), it's awfully hard to deal with this fact of life: *We're all different.*

Sometimes our differences show up physically, sometimes intellectually, sometimes socially. But there are other differences as well. There are differences in personal taste, coordination, social skills, voice control, and attitudes toward art, drama, music, and hundreds of other things.

There are people who try to make a federal case out of these differences. They want to debate which differences are better and which are worse. Arguing about things like that is what stimulates prejudice, racism, and all kinds of other elitist ideas.

Why not just accept the differences? Better yet, why not treasure them as unique gifts from God? He could have stamped everyone out of the same mold, but he didn't. One of the great lessons you can learn in school is that God's decision on differences is OK. You don't have to match everyone and everyone doesn't have to match you.

 Lord, make me different from the world when it comes to sinning. Make me the same as you and your saints when it comes to forgiving. Amen.

Make a point to support and reinforce a friend who likes to do some things you don't. Let them know their way is OK with you.

■ GROWING UP IN SCHOOL: LESSON THREE

1 Kings 19:9-14: "A voice said to him, 'Elijah, what are you doing here?'" (v. 13).

Elijah thought he knew the intent and will of the Lord for his life. That's what got him so upset. Based on his perception, he thought he was a failure. Instead of gathering an ever-growing band of followers, it looked to him like he was the only one left who was loyal—and the outlaws were after him! In fear and disgust he hid until God came after him with a simple question: "What are you doing here?" He wanted Elijah to realize his mistaken judgment and get back to work. Elijah thought he had done his best and failed. God didn't think so. He said, "Get busy. Try some more."

One of the problems everyone faces at school is that we always think we're doing the best we can! It could be true, but more than likely it's not. As the years go by you'll do much more than you can now, and do it much better. School is the place for discovering you can do it better. You learn to write two or three drafts of that composition rather than squeak by with one fast job and settle for a B. You'll be tempted to take on an honors project. Why not read two pages more than is required? Push yourself. Forget the sloppy minimal standards of others. Adopt your own. Set high goals. And when you get close, push them higher.

Lord, you gave me your best in Jesus Christ. Help me give my best because I'm his. Amen.

What's your weakest area of study or school activity? Write down what it would take to make a marked improvement. Set a goal. Press toward it.

■ LEARNING HOW TO THINK

1 John 4:1-4: "My dear friends, do not believe all who claim to have the Spirit, but test them to find out if the spirit they have comes from God" (v. 1).

Learn how to think? Absurd. You don't learn how to think—you just do it. If that be so (and I don't believe it is), it's obvious that some know how to think *better* than others. Whether you learn how to think, or how to think better, it's in the schooling process that these abilities are stirred, beefed up, trained, and tried. One of the greatest skills you will develop in school is your ability to think. When you have that skill in hand, you are educated, no matter what your grade. And if you can't think, you have missed the very reason for going to school.

Bishop Hans Lilje valued the thinking process even more. He made it a required Christian skill when he said, "The two greatest tasks of the church to the people of the church are these: 1) to help Christians see that, at the heart of every decision in life, there is a basic Christian question, and 2) to make Christians think." What do you think about that?

Good thinking happens best when stimulated by much information, much observation, much concentration, and much Christian commitment. Check these things out in yourself.

 What marvelous gifts are our brains, dear Lord. Who but a god would think of a blessing like that. Who but our God did! We praise you. Amen.

How good a thinker are you? Set aside five minutes a day to exclusively think about the largest problem you face. Now concentrate! Look out for the results!

■ WHERE AM I GOING?

Exod. 3:1-10: "Now I am sending you to the king of Egypt so that you can lead my people out of his country" (v. 10).

God knew where the children of Israel were going as they plunged out into the wilderness. He knew not only where, but by what route and when they would get there. He had the goals set. He had revealed these goals to Moses and others—that's why Israel was also called the Promised Land. It was specifically foretold!

No one gets very far in life without specific goals. If there are no goals, there can be no plan of preparation, no system of study, no development of direction. If you don't know where you are going, you also don't know how close you are to getting there! Life then becomes a pointless wandering. It's like following a map with no direction markers, no scale of distance, no familiar outlines.

A lot of kids have maps like that. They have no goals. I guess they think goals fall out of the sky and hit them on the head. No way. Goals are chosen (by you). They can be changed (by you). They may never be achieved (by you), but goals give life direction (for you).

God had a goal for his creation. You can read about his goal for you in Eph. 1:3-12 and lots of other places in the Bible. Now, what are your goals?

Give me a goal, Lord. Better yet, brighten my mind that I may choose a goal which will meet with your approval and fit my needs. Amen.

Set an achievable goal for yourself in three areas: sports, family relations, study. Now "think" (remember yesterday) how you will achieve each. Keep a record of progress. When you reach your goal, buy yourself a Coke and set a new and larger goal.

■ PICK YOUR STAR—CAREFULLY

Matt. 2:1-12: "And so they left, and on their way
they saw the same star they had seen in the East.
. . . It went ahead of them until it stopped
over the place where the child was" (vv. 9-10).

There were a lot of stars in the sky the night the
Wise Men started on their trip to Bethlehem. If they
had picked the wrong one, they might have ended up
discovering America! Instead they let themselves be
led to the greatest thing in the world: their Savior.

There are lots of "stars" for you to follow in life too.
Yesterday I called those "stars" goals. You need to
have goals, to press toward them, but you need to
be very careful how you choose your goals too.

One way to choose a goal is to test whether it is
of God. A goal of becoming the strongest kid on the
block so that everyone will be afraid of you and do
what you want is a lousy Christian goal! It's not of
God. God's Word and Christ's example will help you
evaluate your goals.

But there are three other standards a good goal
must meet. A genuine goal must be *specific* ("I want
to get good enough at tennis to make the team" rather
than "I want to do something athletic"), *measurable*
("I want to get at least three A's," rather than "I want
to get better grades"), and *attainable* (possible for
you, not "I want to become king of Albania").

God gives us skills to select goals. Use them.

Help me find the right star, Lord, and then give
me your kind of strength to follow it. Amen.

**Review your work of yesterday. Make your goals
specific, measurable, and attainable. Then give
yourself a Coke and french fries when you achieve
any of them—fully and honestly.**

■ WHAT YOU NEED IS SOME ADVICE

1 Sam. 3:2-18: ". . . so [Eli] said to [Samuel], 'Go back to bed; and if he calls you again, say, "Speak, Lord. Your servant is listening." ' So Samuel went back to bed" (v. 9).

Many people who offer advice don't seem to be too concerned with you or your problem. They just like to give advice. To further complicate things, most of us don't want to take their advice—even if it turns out to be right. That's dumb, but it's true. So what can we do?

Do like Samuel. Don't listen to just any advice. Find someone you are willing to listen to and *ask* them for advice. Make the first move yourself. Find a good source for assistance and go there. Often you'll choose someone older—a kind of personal Eli.

Then listen to the advice, even if you don't like what you are hearing. Don't spend the advising moments thinking up answers and arguments that would overcome the suggestion. After you've really heard, think before deciding on your path of action. Most decisions can wait at least a little while longer. Take time to let the advice sink in. *Then* make your decision. Make haste slowly.

Among those to whom you should go for advice is your oldest friend, your Father in heaven. He has lots of advice. It's always good—and good for you.

Surround me with people who can advise me, Lord. Give me eager ears, willing to listen, especially to the advice that you give. Amen.

What's the best advice you ever got from an older person? Did you thank your advisor? Ever gone back for more?

■ LOOK OUT LIFE! HERE I COME!

Phil. 4:12-13: "I have the strength to face all conditions by the power that Christ gives me" (v. 13).

There's no less effective approach to life than waiting for something to happen. Sometimes you wait in vain. Other times the things that you passively let happen are not what you wanted or needed at all. Such an approach is occasionally a blessing, but most of the time it's a burden. So do just the opposite: Attack life! Get in there. Don't back away.

Life's lazy ones like to mask their lackadaisical attitude by calling it modesty. Maybe that's true, but the letters I get suggest that the more common reason for casualness is fear—fear of failure, fear of rejection, fear of peer responses. When confronted with those fears, many of us freeze. We try to blend into the woodwork, melt into the crowd.

Don't do that. Get in there. Take a chance. Put your ability on the line. Risk. At the very least, you'll be learning. Usually you'll discover you have more ability than you realized. You'll also discover that most people are not born with ability; they work hard. Capable people are capable because they took the limited talent they were given and developed it. Do the same. Put your hand in Christ's, and make your move—with him.

 I say I'm shy and modest and not the pushy type. I know that's only partly true. The real truth is I'm nervous and afraid. Help me make my move, Lord. Help me try my wings. Amen.

Make a list of things you'd like to do but don't because you are frozen by fear. Select one and try. Go ahead. Then, when we meet, you buy *me* a Coke. I deserve it for the great advice.

■ OUR WORLD IS RUN BY CAESARS

Luke 2:1-3: "In those days Caesar Augustus issued a decree that a census should be taken of the entire Roman world" (v. 1 NIV).

You might as well know it from the start: There's always a Caesar floating around somewhere. You can tell because you hear them ordering people around. They don't instruct or ask, like moms or dads do. Caesars always sound like I'm-in-charge-here-so-let's-do-it-my-way-even-though-it-may-be-wrong. Caesars don't reason; they rule. And there are a lot of them.

So here's two important lessons. One: There will always be certain people in the world who are "in charge." Caesar sent Mary and Joseph off on a long trip from Nazareth to Bethlehem because he was in charge. He ordered. They went. Two: Those people aren't always right. What Caesar didn't know as he stomped around was that God was using *him.*

If you don't know this about the world, you begin expecting things from the world which the world can't give. More than that, you lose your temper and start resisting the world because it's imperfect. There's a better approach: Recognize the world for what it can do—and what it can't. Then rejoice in your heavenly Father who bears no such flaw. He's always right—and on your side.

 I expect so much from the world, Lord, and it has so little to give. Help me recognize its weaknesses and find in them cause to search out your strength. Amen.

What "Caesar" is working on your life? Think about what you can do to keep him from getting you down.

■ WHY NOT HELP THE WORLD IMPROVE?

Dan. 1:1-21: "These four knew ten times more than any fortune-teller or magician" (v. 20).

It's not just that if you can't whip 'em you ought to join 'em. That way's too easy. It's more like, if they aren't right, you ought to do what you can to help them get their act together. How's that for a different approach to the world? That's how Daniel and his three pals decided to deal with their world. They stood their ground on what they considered a moral issue (the food), but applied themselves so that they became ten times smarter than anyone else. How might that approach work for you?

Think of ways in which this world's Caesars bother you. Don't just gripe about them. Help change happen! Are the laws that affect young people unfair? Prepare to be a lawyer or a legislator so you can turn things around. How about the uneven distribution of food and wealth in the world? How about the inequities old folks face? Do those things trouble you? Get with it. Commit yourself to help your world change! To do that, you have to stir up the will within yourself, develop the skills, secure the training, and get ready.

Remember God's charge in Gen. 1:28? Decide to help the world improve. It's your job, from him.

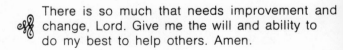 There is so much that needs improvement and change, Lord. Give me the will and ability to do my best to help others. Amen.

If you are going to help the world change, what kinds of training will you need? Name two things you can do right now. Do them.

■ I'VE BEEN WASHED

Titus 3:3-8: ". . . he saved us. It was not because of any good deeds that we ourselves had done, but because of his own mercy that he saved us, through the Holy Spirit, who gives us new birth and new life by washing us" (v. 5).

A dear friend of mine who spent some time in New Guinea among the headhunters told me about a tribe that had been converted to Christianity, been baptized, and were then invited to celebrate a non-Christian feast—just like they always had. Their answer? "We can't. We've been washed."

Have you been washed? Washed in Christ? If you have, then you know right away there are a number of things you shouldn't do. It's not that you shouldn't do them and others may—no one should. The difference is that, as a Christian, you *know* you shouldn't do them. Read Eph. 2:3-10. That opens your eyes to what's new in your life as a child of God and what needs rejection as part of the old way.

Growing up and *growing up as a Christian* are not the same thing. Christians recognize great changes that have taken place in their lives. For us, the phrase "I've been washed" also means "I've been changed." That's what our brothers and sisters in New Guinea realized. That's what Christians of every age have always known.

Jeremiah said it: Turn me and I will be turned. So do it, Lord, and let me have the spiritual maturity to know it has been done—and what that means. Amen.

Determine the day of your baptism. Circle it on your calendar and in some way make it special. Find out who were your sponsors. Pray for them.

■ SLIPPED! AND SLIPPED AGAIN!

Luke 15: "I will get up and go to my father and say, 'Father, I have sinned against God and against you'" (v. 18).

It always seems to surprise Christians that they sin. Some seem to think that if they hold their mouths just right or if they try super-special hard or if they really and truly want to, they can avoid sinning entirely. Not so.

Just so we understand each other, let's make it clear. We are all sinners. Every last one of us *revolts against God, rebels* against his will and intent, *makes mistakes,* and sadly *misses the mark* God has set for us. (In that last sentence are the four meanings of the word *sin* in Scripture.)

It's important that you recognize your sinfulness. It helps you better evaluate yourself, and it gives you a more dependable gauge for evaluating others. More than that, it helps you recognize the enormity of the forgiveness which God has offered to each of us in Christ. Recognition of personal sinfulness is the doorway of understanding through which we walk to catch a glimmer of the meaning of mercy and grace and peace and righteousness. It's the starting point, not the end.

> Lord, I sometimes view my sinfulness as if it were a minor facial flaw needing a bit of spiritual Clearasil. Let me recognize my condition more fully, but be sure I see beyond that reality to your larger truth of forgiveness.

Make a list of your most obvious sins. Use the catechism or the Bible (Exodus 20 and Matthew 5 are a couple places to look) to help your listing. Hide the results where no one but you and God will know.

■ A BETTER WAY OF FACING THE FACTS

Matt. 9:1-8: "Some people brought to him a paralyzed man, lying on a bed. When Jesus saw how much faith they had, he said to the paralyzed man, 'Courage, my son! Your sins are forgiven'" (v. 2).

Some folks can't face the fact of sin because they don't know what to do next! Deny their sins? Laugh? Cry? Look embarrassed? Act casual? What?

Other folks can face the fact of their sin. They know it is a reality of their life. They painfully recognize the effects of their errors and faults. They have a keen appreciation of their darker side and admit they are fully capable of doing anything—if the circumstances are right. They know all that, but they know one thing more: Jesus Christ came and died on the cross to forgive their very real sins.

The word *forgive* is a great one. It doesn't mean forget! If only that which was forgotten was forgiven, there wouldn't be much personal peace in this world. No, the word *forgive* means these things: 1) cover over, 2) send away, 3) let go. In the narrowest sense *only* God forgives. He's the only one who can cover over and send away and let go—and he does. More than that, he broadens the meaning to include me. Because he forgives me, I can pass that forgiveness on to others and release them from the genuine guilt and promised punishment of sin. Read John 20:21-23.

There's no greater message, Lord, than "Your sins are forgiven." Thanks for sending that message to me. Help me share it. Amen.

Remember yesterday's list? Find it. If you want forgiveness for all that is on it, ask God for that blessing. Then destroy the list. God does.

■ SOMETHING SWEETER THAN HONEY

Ps. 119:97-104: "How sweet is the taste of your instructions—sweeter even than honey!" (v. 103).

You know I haven't been making things up, don't you? You're aware that the pages of this book are filled to overflowing with the truth, aren't you? But these words are not just advice from an older Christian, or sayings that have stood the test of time, or an accumulation of life's learnings. This book finds its facts and inspiration in the Scriptures, God's revelation. Anything within these pages that does not find its source there isn't worth very much. So says the author! So, also, say the people of God of every age. Christians treasure the Word. They read it, learn it, study it, search it for deeper meaning, believe its message.

The best message the Scriptures contain is that of our salvation in Jesus Christ. (Paul agreed with that. Read 2 Tim. 3:15.) As a matter of fact, that's really all the message there is. Everything in one way or another relates to God's plan of salvation for all people. Don't ever forget that one of those "all people" is you!

Isn't it time to get more serious about the way you use the Bible? It's God's book for you.

Let your Word guide me, Lord. By your Holy Spirit give me the wisdom to recognize and treasure the truth of the Scriptures. Give me a commitment to read your Word daily. That would be a great gift. Amen.

Look for some "honey." Read the following and underline the sweetest parts: 1 Corinthians 13, John 3, Ephesians 1, Psalm 130. Search for the spiritual sweet stuff.

■ HOME FOR SUPPER

1 Cor. 10:16-17: "The cup which we use in the Lord's Supper and for which we give thanks to God: when we drink from it, we are sharing in the blood of Christ. And the bread we break: when we eat it, we are sharing in the body of Christ" (v. 16).

Baptism—the Scriptures—the Lord's Supper. Many Christians call those three "the means of grace." That means they are the avenues or the pipelines or the channels by which God's grace comes to his people. Each is treasured highly, but each is used differently. Baptism is a once-in-a-lifetime event. Use of the Scriptures should be a daily experience. But what about the Lord's Supper? How is it best used? And how often?

The Lord's Supper has a number of valuable uses. It is a way in which we remember the Lord and his sacrifices on our behalf. More than that, trusting in his promised real presence in the wine and wafer, we receive the forgiveness of our sins. The Lord's Supper is also a way to express and strengthen our connectedness with each other. We are not alone. We are family. We are *God's* family, fed and nourished at the table he has prepared.

When's the last time you were home for supper?

 What nice names for such a nice thing, Father: the Lord's Supper, the Table of the Lord, Communion. Thanks for preparing the event and inviting me. I'll be there—every time I can. Amen.

Check out your catechism, or ask your pastor, how to prepare to receive the Lord's Supper. Get ready for the next time it's available.

■ IT'S HIS CHURCH

Eph. 5:25-32:   ". . . for we are members of his body" (v. 30).

Every congregation I've ever been in can tell you the day of their church's dedication. A dedication means that the building and all its furnishings are given over to God. The people who dedicated the building waive their right of ownership. It's God's. When people are ready to make public commitment to Christ, they join a congregation. The congregation they join is an association of people who have also given themselves to Christ.

By the time you get the committed people and the dedicated buildings together, it might just dawn on you that "going to a church" or "joining a church" or "belonging to a church" are all ways of describing your relationship to Christ! If you are mad at the church, you are really mad at Christ. If you ignore the church, or quit the church, or serve the church, or build the church, or whatever you do in relation to a Christian church, you do it *with, to, at, by, in* Christ! It's all his. Now do you see what makes church so important? Church is important because Christ is!

 Protect your church, O Lord. It is yours. As a matter of fact, it is you. So take care of yourself, Lord, for my sake. Amen.

List five things that are right with your church and that please you.

■ SURE THERE ARE HYPOCRITES

Rom. 8:1-11: "But you do not live as your human nature tells you to; instead, you live as the Spirit tells you to—if, in fact, God's Spirit lives in you. Whoever does not have the Spirit of Christ does not belong to him" (v. 9).

What is a hypocrite? Well, for one thing, it's not something people like to be called. The literal meaning of the word *hypocrite* is "an actor." Hypocrites are actors. They play a part. Their way of doing things is not real for them. They seem to be one thing, but are actually very different.

Some people say they stay away from the church (remember what that is?) because there are hypocrites in the congregation. They are right—the church is full of hypocritical sinners. It better be! The very purpose of the church is to help them. How can you help them if there are none in the church?

When serious and committed people talk about hypocrites in the church, they mean that the people of God don't always act as honorably and helpfully as they should. That's absolutely true. But that's not the last word. Hypocrites, too, can go to Christ for forgiveness—and receive it. I know. I do it all the time.

Don't be too hard on hypocrites, friend. You're only hard on yourself. Anyone who says he or she isn't a hypocrite is just acting. And we know what *that* word means.

God, be merciful to me, a sinner. I can't say it any better, Lord. I'm glad I don't have to, and that you are. Amen.

Take a good hard look at your "acting" ability. When do you feel like a hypocrite? What can you do to change the things that make you feel that way?

73

■ WHAT DOES A PASTOR DO ANYWAY?

John 10:11-16: "I am the good shepherd, who is willing to die for the sheep" (v. 11).

The word *pastor* means "shepherd." A pastor is someone who takes care of a flock of sheep or, in our instance, people. Jesus claimed the title for himself and, in so doing, set a standard for the conduct of pastors in his church that is impossible to beat—or even meet. But you get an idea of how a pastor should live and work by using Jesus as a model and his specific words as patterning resolutions.

Good shepherds take tender care of their flocks. The flocks don't always fully know about or appreciate the quality of care they receive. But a flock must recognize the need for a shepherd and, also, know the care a shepherd of Christ should be giving. In that way, the flock can either compliment the shepherd or remind the pastor of responsibilities ignored.

How's it going with you and your pastor? Do you know and understand what your pastor does? For you? Don't be too quick to scoot by these questions. Only as you understand what the pastor is called to do can you determine that yours is a faithful shepherd and bless the Lord for that gift to you. The pastor is called by God to tend the flock in the style of Christ—nothing more, nothing less.

 It's great that you call pastors into your service, Lord. Thanks for ours. Help me to be a better sheep and easier to lead. Amen.

Pastors preach, teach, counsel, conduct worship, and administer. Tell your pastor thanks, in person or in a note.

74

■ THE LITTLE BOAT AND THE STORMY SEA

Matt. 8:23-27: "Then he got up and ordered the winds and the waves to stop, and there was a great calm" (v. 26).

One of the oldest symbols of the church is that of a boat. A lot of religious books and stained glass windows contain that symbol. Anytime you see a sailboat with a cross on its mainsail, that's a symbol of the church. But why?

For one reason, the church is made up of people who have been held up and supported by water, just like boats are. Boats are supported by water. So are Christians. Check that in 1 Peter 3:18-22.

I think another reason the ship is such an appropriate picture is that all boats leak a little. That makes sailors nervous. More than that, the ship's natural surrounding is the often stormy and powerful sea. Those two conditions put any ship in constant danger of sinking! I can't think of any more appropriate picture of the church than a ship—lots of storms outside, lots of leaks inside.

Yes, the church floats. About the time a storm appears ready to destroy the craft, God stills the waves and plugs the leaks and keeps all safe. That's what our church is like. We'd sure be in trouble without him!

 Keep stilling the storms, Father. Use me to plug the leaks. Allow us to float in peace kept by your grace and mercy. Amen.

What's the largest "leak" in your local parish? What can you do to plug it? In the meanwhile, can you at least sail?

75

■ A COMMUNITY OF THE REDEEMED

Acts 2:43-47: ''And every day the Lord added to their group those who were being saved'' (v. 47).

Groucho Marx once declined to join a club by saying, "I refuse to join a club that would have a man like me as a member!" When I look at my own church, I'm tempted to resign for the same reasons. I can't believe someone like me can qualify as a member of the Christian church and the community which it represents. Am I the reason the pattern of action which the earliest Christian community established, and which is reported in the Acts, is so very different from what I seem to see in my congregation?

The basic qualification for membership in the church is not that a person is perfect, but that a person is redeemed. Redeemed means "bought again" or "bought back." People in the church have all been bought back by Christ Jesus. Those who do not believe this are some of those hypocrites we talked about earlier. But that's not the case with his confessing redeemed! They are out in the open, admitting their own sinfulness and praising God for his saving activity in Christ.

Now take another look at your church. Empowered by the Holy Spirit, those forgiven sinful people could do more, and, hopefully, they will. But the momentary miracle is that they do as much as they do!

It's so nice to be surrounded by people who are just like me, and then have all of us surrounded by a God like you. Thanks for bringing me into the community. Amen.

List 10 people in your church who you respect and would like to imitate. Tell any one of them how you feel.

■ THE CHRISTIAN COMMUNITY HELPS

Acts 20:32-38: ". . . remembering the words that the Lord Jesus himself said, 'There is more happiness in giving than in receiving' " (v. 35).

The Bible is filled with stories about God's people and how they acted. Especially meaningful are the stories that come from the New Testament which tell the history of how the early Christians acted. One thing is clear in those chronicles: The early church cared for and helped those in need—and the "helpers" weren't that much better off than the "helped"!

As a member of the Christian community, you can get help. But, as part of the Christian church, you can and ought to give help too. Maybe this will all make better sense to you after you have searched and found the answers to these questions:

1. What help does my congregation provide for me and what does it cost in money and effort to give it to me?

2. What does my congregation provide for others in our parish and what does it cost in money and effort to provide that?

3. What does my congregation do in our immediate community, in our state or province, in our country, and in the world, and what does that require in money and effort?

Help me see I'm helped. Help me help, Lord. Amen.

Make sure you answer the three questions. Get the facts.

■ NO PRIVATE RELIGION

Eph. 2:19-22: ". . . you are now fellow citizens with God's people and members of the family of God" (v. 19).

I don't have to go to church and be with other people. I can worship God all by myself." Wrong!

You can't always worship God all by yourself. Were he to speak directly to you in your private meditation, he would say, "What are you doing here? Where's the rest of the family I gave you?" We are not single sheep chasing around where we wish; we are part of his appointed flock.

The earlier you get that understanding of the church firmly planted in your mind, the sooner you will achieve God's intent for you among his people. We have been linked together in love by him. Do not disconnect yourself. Do not allow others to think they can detach themselves from the family and still live. His messages of mercy come to each of us *through other people.* To separate yourself from his people is to separate yourself from God.

I can't say it better than this: "Let us . . . help one another to show love and to do good. Let us not give up the habit of meeting together, as some are doing. Instead, let us encourage one another all the more . . ." (Heb. 10:24-25). Those are powerful and pointed words. Pay attention to them.

I get so self-centered, Lord, and so quickly lose my perspective of concern for others. Keep me in a responsible relationship with you and yours. Amen.

Lay back a bit and reflect on the fact that the church is God's family of faith. Focus on the word *family.* What thoughts come to your mind?

■ CHRIST—THE CHURCH'S GLUE

Col. 3:8-15: ". . . but Christ is all, Christ is in all" (v. 11).

Every Sunday morning, God's people see a miracle happen again. They see people coming to church. It *is* amazing. The church is the only voluntary organization in the world which regularly gathers in large numbers on a weekly basis. Read that last sentence again and test it out, word for word. It's true! With every other organization, there are either irregular meetings or people don't gather in large numbers or it isn't voluntary or there is no structure. But the church? The church is different. It breaks all those "rules" of the world. Against all odds and predictions and norms, it does its thing.

Why? What gives the church this strange and fascinating capacity to do the impossible? The answer is known to all Christians: Jesus Christ. The church is *more* than an organization; *more* than voluntary; *more* than human. It is the very body of Christ. All of us individually are part of that special unit collectively. We know that. But the glue that keeps us stuck on each other (and stuck on God's way) is the Lord.

"I am the church! You are the church! We are the church together!" Those lines are part of a delightful song written by Richard Avery and Donald Marsh (Hope Publishing Company). Learn it. Sing it. Be it. Christ wants it that way. He glues us together.

Keep us united, Lord, just like you intended. Let us be one. Amen.

Find out how many people make the miracle happen at your church each Sunday. See if you can't increase the number some way.

■ FEELINGS CAN FOOL YOU

John 10:17-21: "But others were saying, 'A man with a demon could not talk like this! How could a demon give sight to blind people?' " (v. 21).

I get lots of letters from young people asking about feelings. Specifically the letters are usually about their not having certain kinds of feelings or having feelings they don't want or understand. Both problems bother them because somewhere along the line they have been convinced that feelings are a dependable guide and a consistent monitor of all that is right and all that is wrong. Not so!

Some days I don't "feel" very spiritual or loved or worthy. Some days I don't "feel" what I am doing is worthwhile or appreciated or effective. Some days I don't "feel" particularly parental or pastoral or married. But whether I feel that way or not, I *am* spiritual, loved, and worthy. And I do things that are worthwhile, appreciated, and effective. And I am a parent, a pastor, and a partner in marriage. I am those things *even when I don't feel like it!*

Feelings can fool you. Check them out against the facts. You *have been* forgiven. That's a fact. God *does* love you. That's a fact. You *are* cared for. That's a fact. Feelings *can* fool. That's a fact.

When I'm having trouble with my feelings, Lord, let your Spirit impress on me the facts I need to know. Give me power to believe them, please. Amen.

Page through your hymnbook for songs that state the facts of the Christian faith. When feelings fool you, whistle or sing one of those hymns. Pick out a favorite and memorize it. It's easy.

■ BE A BIBLE STUDENT

John 5:31-40: "You study the Scriptures, because you think that in them you will find eternal life. And these very Scriptures speak about me!" (v. 39).

Jesus wasn't just encouraging the people to read the Bible when he spoke the words of our scripture reference; he was stating a fact. They *were* searching the Scriptures. The trouble is they didn't recognize the real meaning of the words. They didn't understand the clear references to Jesus as Savior and Lord in the Word. But just because they couldn't see didn't mean the message wasn't there!

The words of Christ in the Bible reference above teach at least two things to thinking Christians. First, they clearly say that searching the Scriptures is a worthwhile and important Christian function. So don't act as if you didn't really know whether you ought to do it or not. Hear his encouragement.

Second, we are told to dig out the meaning of the words in the Word. That's not as hard to do as you may think. Jesus gave a clue. Look for him. Look for him everywhere in the Scriptures. He keeps popping up. If you need help for the searching, it's all around you—in your congregation, through resources like people and many excellent books. So get busy digging through the Word. It will connect you with fellow Christians and with Christ. He's a treasure worth the seeking—and finding.

Lord, I'm often so lazy about my study of the Scriptures. Put me in the midst of Christians who hunger and thirst after your Word and who can infect me with the same yearnings. Amen.

Join a Bible class at your church. If there is none, start one.

■ THE CHURCH DOES WHAT IT'S TOLD

Acts 1:6-11: "But when the Holy Spirit comes upon you, you will be filled with power, and you will be witnesses for me . . ." (v. 8).

Sharing the Christian faith is one of the most important tasks the local congregation performs. It's even more important (Is *that* possible?) in the daily life of the individual Christian. Even knowing that, Christians still have trouble fulfilling this responsibility they are given by the Lord. The reason? They don't know what witnessing means.

Witnessing doesn't mean arguing with someone about the things you believe. It's not witnessing when you hassle people or intimidate them. That's not Christian witnessing—not at all!

Witnessing is a very personal activity. It starts with you. A witness is someone who personally sees or experiences something and tells about it. There's always an "eye" and an "I" in Christian witnessing.

Convincing people they are wrong and you are right is hard work and is seldom accomplished. God didn't give you *that* task. All he asks you to do is simply state before others the things that have happened in your life since you came to Christ! He, then, blesses your words with the Holy Spirit and does the work of changing people. We need only do what he told us: Witness.

Lord Jesus, I keep making things so much tougher than they really are. Help me to keep it simple by just doing what you have told me to do. Amen.

Pick someone you know who needs a Christian witness. Make it. Check out how well your church is organized to witness.

■ SERVING MEANS HELPING YOUR BROTHER

Gen. 4:3-9: "The Lord asked Cain, 'Where is your brother Abel?' " (v. 9).

Cain never understood how he should treat Abel. He forgot that Abel was his brother. "Am I my brother's keeper?" he asked. Of course not, Cain. You are your brother's brother. Can you see the difference?

Congregations who care are always aware that they have needy brothers and sisters. The Bible is full of that kind of concern. James says that genuine religion consists of visiting the widows and orphans in their suffering and keeping yourself from being corrupted by the world (James 1:27). You can't walk very far in the Word before you see how impossible it is to say, "Our church is concerned with the spiritual needs of the people, not their physical and social requirements!" That kind of division is impossible! People come with all the parts connected.

So what about feeding the hungry and looking out for the interests of the elderly, the poor, and the handicapped? That's the church's business too! And how about some concern for the jobless, the emotionally disturbed, the economically deprived? That's also the work of the church. Christians in and through the church have been saying for centuries that they are their brothers' brothers and are fully responsible for all of the family's needs. What do you say?

Put a concern for all people on my heart, Lord, and give me a will to help them. Amen.

Do something about someone's physical need. Find a place to put in two hours work—and another place to give a few dollars—and do it.

■ THE EARLIEST RESPONSIBILITY GOD GIVES YOU

Matt. 19:19: ". . . you shall love your neighbor as yourself."

Somewhere in the shuffle of growing up, people forget (or maybe they are taught to forget) that the person you are most accountable for in life is you. No one knows you the way you know you. No one sees your little deceptions and proud pettiness the way you do. No one senses your needs and hopes and yearnings like you do. No one is as fully accountable for your care and your nurture as you are. Jesus thinks caring for self is so obvious that he suggests you treat others with the same tenderness you show yourself!

But how do you keep giving primary care to yourself from getting out of hand? How do you prevent egotism and stifle self-centeredness?

You deal with those things by recognizing them for what they are. Those distortions of Christ's intent aren't blessings; they are burdens you ought refuse. They don't build your you. They stain and flaw what you want and need for yourself. Don't allow those erosive characteristics to take control. Instead, shift your focus to others and play the words of Christ both ways: Love your neighbor as yourself/love yourself as you do your neighbor. That way there's always lots of care for everyone—for you and all those around you.

 Lord, I need to see that loving others is really loving myself. Thanks for establishing the model I try to reflect. Amen.

With conscious intent and as an act of appreciation to God, do something nice for yourself that won't hurt others and which will help you grow.

■ THE REAL ME

1 Cor. 15:3-11: "But by God's grace I am what
I am . . ." (v. 10).

St. Paul had a very clear picture of himself. He had
an even clearer picture of what he was because of
God's work in him. He recognized he made mistakes,
and he knew how to take those mistakes to the cross
of Christ for forgiveness and renewal. He knew all
that about himself. What do you know about yourself?

As you answer that, please realize not all people
are alike. Not even all good people are alike. Even
caring Christians who walk by faith come with
significant variations. They might see the world from
different perspectives. They value people and events
in different ways. Yet they all love their Lord, trust
in the effectiveness of his grace and of the faith God
gives, and rely on the witness of the Word. They
have much in common, but they also have many
differences.

People don't always have to be wrong if they differ
from you—or you from them. That's the way God
made us. Don't force people into a single mold. And
don't let others turn you into a "cookie-cutter
Christian," identical to every other. Keep your
specialness. God gave it to you.

By your grace I have all the specialness I need.
Help me claim your uniqueness for me by the
Spirit. Amen.

**Write a description of yourself. Read it over. Sharpen
it up every day for a week. Is that you?**

■ LIVING WITH LAWS

Rom. 13:1-7: "Everyone must obey state authorities, because no authority exists without God's permission, and the existing authorities have been put there by God" (v. 1).

Every year on National Law Day, lawyers in the United States celebrate that ours is a nation governed by laws, not by people. That means the law of the land doesn't keep changing depending on your age, your social condition, your race, or the mood of the judge. Even if a citizen gets a raw deal at one court, he or she can appeal to a higher court for justice.

The existence of laws guarantees there will be no accepted abuse. It's a fact that policemen stop teenage drivers more often than those of other ages, often with less cause. That's not fair. But a lot of caring judges work hard at correcting that kind of improper application of the law. They realize that, even with laws, there are instances of injustice, but not nearly so many as would be the case if there were no laws! Martin Luther once said that the only thing worse than a bad government (and laws) was no government. The law helps keep peace and protects the weak. It *does* do that more often than not. It would do it even better if we, as Christians, were consistently supportive of the law and more conscious of our responsibilities to uphold and support law and order. Are you willing to do that?

 We praise you as a God of order, Lord. Help us to resist the chaos of lawlessness in the world and bring more order to the life of all. Amen.

List a law that clearly protects you right now. Then list one that you think is unfair. What can you do to support the one and change the other? Think.

■ HERE COMES THAT WORD AGAIN!

1 Cor. 7:29-31: "For this world, as it is now, will not last much longer" (v. 31).

Is there any tougher thing to deal with in life than change? We've already discussed physical changes and changes within your family. But there are more! Just about the time you think you have everything in place and think you know how things ought to be done, along comes change—someone with a new idea, a new rule, or a new way of doing things. Change is a reality in the world, and to deal with it you need to recognize a number of things about it.

1) Not all change is bad. Even though it unsettles you for a while, change can be good. Don't see "changers" as your enemy. Learn to be more flexible. 2) Then again, not all change is good. The new isn't always better than the old. Test things. You've got a basis for judging, remember? There's the Word of God, others' advice, your own experiences. 3) You'll usually survive. People handled change pretty well in the past whether it was the advent of the horseless carriage, the telephone, or jetliners. 4) God won't change in his intent or his commitment of care for you. That's why you'll survive. He gives his angels charge concerning you—daily. Isn't that nice?

The form of this world and everything in it changes, Lord. Will you who do not change abide with me? I'd like it that way. Amen.

Choose the five greatest changes that have taken place in your world since your birth. Which were good and which were bad?

■ THANKS FOR THE CHANGE, LORD!

1 Cor. 13:11: "When I was a child, my speech, feelings, and thinking were all those of a child; now that I am a man, I have no more use for childish ways."

The last devotion and the next few all have to do with the world and change and you—all three. The world is in flux. Change is a reality. You are in motion too. Life can be like trying to hit a moving target from a high-speed roller coaster using a cracked bow and a bent arrow! But don't think that you are the only one facing turmoil and rapid change. Everyone does.

While change in the world may or may not be good, all change within you that meshes with the Word and will of God is good. It shows you are making moves from that childish condition we mentioned earlier to becoming an increasingly mature adult—a genuine woman, a complete man.

Take your "you" out into that dynamic world without worry. Go ahead. God is equipping you to act in a better way with a fuller realization of how the world acts too. As a child, you couldn't do much about the world. As a godly grown-up, you're ready for it!

Lord, I know I am changing. The old wasn't all that good and the new isn't bad. Stick with me. Help me make the moves I need to. Amen.

What's the most "childish" thing you need to give up in order to make it in the world? How can you do that?

■ CHOICES

Matt. 27:15-26: "So when the crowd gathered, Pilate asked them, 'Which one do you want me to set free for you? Jesus Barabbas or Jesus called the Messiah?' " (v. 17).

Do you know what you meet when your changing "you" moves out into a changing world? I'll tell you. You meet choices.

Children don't have many choices. What's to choose about taking a nap right after lunch or waiting 15 minutes? But adults get choices. As you become more adult, you get more choices.

Sometimes the choices are easy decisions between things that are clearly wrong and other things that are clearly right! (Shall I steal a record or shall I not?) Sometimes the choices are tougher decisions between better and best. (Shall I buy the green blouse with the ruffle or the white one with the bow?) Sometimes the choice is only between bad and worse! (Shall I take the painful series of shots or hope the dog that bit me wasn't rabid?)

The best way for dealing with choices is to quickly make all those which God's clear command or your neighbor's obvious need requires. Look for help and good advice in making other more difficult decisions. Pray over every decision, asking that God's will be done in and through you. You'll be surprised how much easier the choosing process becomes!

> Lord, I'm glad you never hesitate in making key choices where I am concerned. Help me be like you. Together with you, I know I will make the right choices. Amen.

What's the last choice you made? How well did you do? Give yourself a score.

◼ YOU MUST MAKE UP YOUR MINDS

1 Kings 18:20-40: "How much longer will it take you to make up your minds?" (v. 21).

An important thing to know about choices is that they *must* finally be made. You can't keep bumping along, avoiding the time of determination, in the hope that the problem will disappear. It usually won't. You must finally make key decisions before your reluctance pulls you under!

But how do you do it? How do you decide—correctly? Try this six-step process: 1) Accurately determine what you are trying to decide. 2) Develop all the possible solutions you can. 3) Pick the best one. 4) Put it to work. *Do* what you choose. 5) Evaluate how things are working out. 6) If you see it isn't working as you hoped, go back to step one and start again.

That's an effective process for decision making. It will help you make up your mind and lead you to a decision. You will be able to evaluate the decision you have reached and change it if and when that is needed. But the key to it all is a determination to make up your mind. Without that, nothing will happen—at least not by your choice. When choosing seems tough, remember that God made up his mind about us. He decided that he wanted you, no matter the cost. What a wonderful decision!

 Lord, help me make up my mind when it is necessary. Guide me to right choices and give me courage to make them. Amen.

Apply the six steps listed above to the concern in your life which needs most attention right now.

■ WHAT ABOUT THE FUTURE?

John 14:1-3: " . . . I will come back and take you to myself, so that you will be where I am" (v. 3).

One thing is certain about the future: Jesus is waiting for you there! The Christ of yesterday and today is also the Christ of tomorrow.

Many people worry about the future. But which future? Actually, there isn't just one. There are three. The first is the *probable future*. That's the future that will appear if you don't do anything, if you just let things roll along. It's easy to predict that future. It's usually dull and flat and blah. It's the future of people who don't like to think about the future.

The second futures are the *possible futures*. That's in the plural because there's not just one road for you to walk; you have many alternatives.

Finally, there is the *preferable future*. That's the future you can choose *after* weighing all the possibilities and factoring in your skills, hopes, and desires. You make decisions about your life today *which shape your future*. For example, if you don't take math this year, you can't enter engineering school next year. See how it works?

Christ not only has the whole world in his hand, but the future of the world as well. Think about it and work toward the future, hand-in-hand with him.

 Tomorrow sometimes scares me, Lord. Keep reminding me that you know my fears and are moving toward my tomorrow with me. Amen.

List three decisions you've made in the past month which will affect your future. Are they as good now as you thought they were then?

■ GO GET A JOB

2 Thess. 3:6-12: ". . . whoever refuses to work is not allowed to eat" (v. 10).

How much thought have you ever given to getting a job? Work is a useful and important part of life, and finding a job is crucial to work. A lot of kids don't know how to go about it. They don't know how to add up their skills and take them to the place where those skills might get the most attention. They don't know how to put their best foot forward and make a positive impression. They don't even know where to look for help. Some even think the world owes them a job. If that's the way you feel, you better reconsider or have a dad that loves his child and owns a business!

If you need some help, try this: Itemize what you can do and what those skills command in the job market. Check your attitude too. Are you willing to exert yourself and give your best? Look in the mirror. Would you want to hire someone who looks like you to serve in a restaurant or sell at a store? Ask someone you trust to give you advice on where to look for work, and when, and how. All that will help.

Work, and the pleasant results of work, are one of God's great blessings. Recognize and bless him for this gift.

Thanks for my job, Lord. If I haven't gotten it yet, thanks for what's coming. Amen.

Go through the want ads and circle four jobs for which you might qualify that look interesting to you. Circle four others that you don't qualify for but which look more interesting to you. What can you do to make yourself eligible?

■ ESCAPING DOESN'T WORK

Ps. 55:5-8: "I wish I had wings like a dove.
I would fly away and find rest" (v. 6).

You and I live in a world filled with personal
problems. We are also surrounded by people who
use all sorts of ways to escape those problems. Some
try drinking. Others use drugs. Some get super busy
and involved. Any method for avoiding reality is like
the psalmist's yearning to sprout wings so that he
could fly away; it doesn't work. Escaping can become
more troublesome than the problem you are seeking
to avoid.

It's not that Christians never yearn to escape. Many
Christians ache for relief from their problems and
temptations. But the wiser ones are very careful as
they search for help. There are many legitimate ways
to ease the pressure in life, to relieve a burden or to
calm inner tension. How about sharing with a friend?
Or prayer? Ever made a careful analysis of the
problem? Or sought professional counsel? All of
those approaches are more creative than escaping!

Confront your problem. Face your difficulty
head-on. Get assistance from your friends, your
family, your church. And, most important, talk with
your Father in heaven. He delivers his children from
all kinds of evil.

 Help me face my problems, Lord, and avoid
the kind of escapes which are more
troublesome than the problem I yearn to avoid.
Amen.

**How do you "escape?" Sleep? Other worse things?
Close down one of your favorite escape hatches.
Pick it and plug it.**

■ OOPS! YOUR ATTITUDE IS SHOWING

Gen. 4:6: "Then the Lord said to Cain, 'Why are you angry? Why that scowl on your face?'"

You can read some people like a book. Get a good look at their faces or their postures or listen to their way of speaking and you know what's going on inside them. Your body language, the words you select and the way you say them, the eagerness or anger in your eyes all send messages—so be careful.

Then should you mask your feelings and hide your emotions? What about being honest? Upon closer examination, I think you will find that a lot of so-called honesty is really nothing more than rudeness and bad temper. Polite, sensitive, caring people do not wave their feelings like a flag. People who want to get along do not match another's bad manners with equally poor ones of their own. Sometimes a situation is best served by keeping your peace. A difficult task is more easily done under an overlay of good humor, whether the humor is genuine or a little conjured. To put it simply, each of us does much to create our own attitude, and it shows.

A positive attitude stimulates the same kind of response in others. Try it. You'll see that it's true. It also blocks the blahs and keeps the blues from camping in your heart.

Lord, my attitude often needs improvement. I can't handle it entirely by myself. Encourage me. Make my heart your home. That will make a difference. Amen.

What is your most common demonstrated attitude? Cooperation? Appreciation? Happiness? Concern? A yearn to learn? What would you like it to be?

■ MY COUNTRY!

1 Peter 2:13-17: "For the sake of the Lord submit yourselves to every human authority" (v. 13).

Somewhere along the line, everyone comes to grips with what it means to be a citizen of his or her country. Some cry out, "My country—right or wrong!" Others take the position, "My country—who needs it?"

Christians should recognize their countries as special gifts of God to them, the products of the work of many men and women who walked before them and unique blessings that help set the tone for the world in which they mature.

What do you do if you think your country is in error? If you live in a country where it is possible for citizens to institute change, thank God for that blessing. Then get busy! If you live in a country with more restricted possibilities, you may strive for richer opportunities or work for a better environment or even leave and go where your style of life is more accepted. Many of our parents and grandparents did just those things in the years gone by!

The one position Christians cannot take is unconcern toward their countries. If things aren't right, work to bring them into order. If things are correct, preserve and protect what you see and experience.

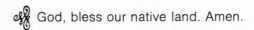 God, bless our native land. Amen.

What can you do for your country? Why not start by volunteering to help someone running for political office. They need people like you.

■ YOU'RE IN THE ARMY NOW

Luke 3:14: "Some soldiers also asked him, 'What about us? What are we to do?'"

There are few generations in the history of any nation that escape some kind of confrontation with war. What does a Christian do when faced with the possibility of being drafted or fighting in a war?

Many Christians recognize a call to military service as an obligation to serve their country which they are willing to accept. Christians have supported the military services from the position that in a sinful world a military force is needed to protect the innocent and keep oppression in check. There are many fine Christians in military services today. They bring a quality of concern and conscientiousness to their commitment that blesses us all.

There are also many Christians who feel they cannot serve in the military. Their position may not totally reject service to their country, but it often does not permit them to fire a weapon at anyone for any reason. Many Christian denominations support the right to take this position and will help young people determine whether theirs are genuine convictions which meet the standards of exception governments allow.

Developing a position toward the draft and military service is not easy. Start giving thought to it now.

 Protect and defend all those who strive to bring order into life, O Lord. Help them keep their humanity. Amen.

What are your present feelings about military service? State your position in no more than five sentences. Discuss it with a friend.

■ LET'S TAKE A BREAK

Mark 6:30-32: "Let us go off by ourselves to some place where we will be alone and you can rest a while" (v. 31).

How about this for a list of great words: picnic, vacation, rest, trip, weekend, ball game, sailing. How many other words could you add that would fit right in? All of them have to do with leisure and recreation. But what do leisure and recreation have to do with God and Christian beliefs?

Taking a break is God's idea. Did you know that Sabbath (as in "Remember the *Sabbath* day to keep it holy") means rest? That's what the word *means*. And whose idea was the Sabbath?

Take a look at the word *recreation*. Break it apart. You have *re* and *creation*. In combination, re-creation means to make again. When you are recreating, you are renewing yourself, refreshing yourself, brightening your outlook and disposition. Most important, you are doing what God desires, and what Jesus exampled.

I'm not going to warn you about overdoing recreation. I think that if you see the divine intent and possibilities in recreating, you won't need such a warning. You'll see recreation as a pleasant ministry to yourself, from God, and as a way of setting a pattern others can profitably and properly follow.

Father, you rested on the seventh day, and your Son followed your will. Help me to see the place of rest and recreation in your plan of things. Amen.

Help someone in your family (mom or dad?) see the importance of recreation and rest. Speak to them about it and plan a time to put God's intent into practice.

■ YOU NEED A HOBBY

Zech. 8:1-8: "And the streets will again be full of boys and girls playing" (v. 5).

Our scripture reading states that one sign of God's reigning presence in life (at least in the life of Jerusalem) is boys and girls playing in the streets. What they are playing is not too important. What's important is that playing is consistent with the will of God. So, let me ask you, "What's your hobby?"

Hobbies are great. Most are also demanding. Try making a delicate model, doing a little gardening, or taking up archery. You'll learn how much effort is required. Hobbies make demands on you and force you to strive for certain goals. Maybe that's why hobbies are also so rewarding. From the day you adopt one, you begin to experience increasingly satisfying results. Every painting looks better. Roller-skating gets more graceful. Collectibles accumulate. Hobbies also help you meet other people and give you something to say when you do. Boys (*all* boys) have trouble talking with girls (and vice versa). With a good hobby, you have something to talk about!

A hobby keeps you occupied and usually out of trouble. It adds quality to your life and brightens the lives of others. No wonder a good hobby makes you feel like you are right in God's plan of things.

 Lead me to a hobby that blesses me, helps others, and causes us to praise your name, Lord. Amen.

Pick a hobby and work hard at it for one week. Before you quit, go talk to someone who shares your choice. You might change your mind.

■ MONEY TALKS—ABOUT YOU

1 Tim. 6:6-10: "For the love of money is a source of all kinds of evil" (v. 10).

Money is fascinating. Look up the word *money* in the encyclopedia. You will see all the odd kinds of money people have used through the ages: stones, gold, nuts, wire, pearls, you name it. At one time or another, almost everything has served as money for some people somewhere. But what is money, really?

Money is nothing more than an easy way for exchanging one kind of service for another. You mow lawns for four hours to get money to buy a record that took someone else the same amount of time to make, ship, and market. That's not fully accurate, but it's close enough to serve my purpose. You see, money is really you. It's your effort and intelligence and ambition turned into paper or silver.

Remember yesterday—about hobbies? I think some people make collecting money their hobby. They go wild about it. Their respect for money and their zeal in accumulating it exceed all common sense. They just *love* money! They will do anything for money. Paul warns them (and us) what will happen—that kind of devotion leads to problems. Just think about things you've seen other kids do for money. Don't let your attitude toward money send out the wrong message about you.

 I'm more precious than silver and gold to you, Lord. May you and your will ever be the same to me. Amen.

Just to help you understand whose the money is, take a look at some coins and bills. Count the indications of God's ownership. Look carefully.

■ I'M SO LONELY I COULD DIE

Ps. 102:1-8: "I lie awake; I am like a lonely bird on a housetop" (v. 7).

Being alone is one thing; being lonely is quite another. God understands loneliness. (Read Gen. 2:18 for his attitude toward loneliness and his creative solution!) People have always experienced the heavy burden of loneliness. (Read Psalm 130.) And are there any lonelier words than Christ's cry from the cross, "My God, my God, why did you abandon me?" (Mark 15:34)? Loneliness is a grim and universal experience. But, good news! There *is* a solution.

When you look for a solution to loneliness (and most people do at some time), start where Christ did. He turned to his Father. That's *your* Father too. Millions have found in the Father a powerful and continuing answer to loneliness. Go to him.

The second approach to loneliness involves the Father too. Go to where the Father's children gather. One of the greater blessings the church gives is relief from loneliness by putting you into contact with other Christians. Hand in hand with them, you won't have time to get lonely!

Look out for other lonelies! Share with them God's one-two punch: Head for the Father and then for the Father's people. You'll never die of loneliness in either place.

Lord, you know about loneliness and you know the secret of overcoming loneliness. Help me imitate you for my own good. Amen.

Who's lonely around you? Take a look. Help them fight those feelings. If you are helping them, they won't be alone anymore—and neither will you.

■ A FULL TUMMY IN A HUNGRY WORLD

Prov. 28:27: "Give to the poor and you will never
be in need. If you close your eyes to the poor,
many people will curse you."

There's little that captured the concern of the Lord
more than the needs of people. He healed the sick,
fed the hungry, and raised people from the dead.

In today's world there isn't much that you can do
to overcome disease—not without a medical education
—so that's out for most of us. And I don't know of
anyone but Jesus who can raise people from the dead.
That leaves feeding the hungry, but that's right down
our alley. All it takes is a will.

People are hungry. In much of Africa, some parts
of Europe and North America, and large sections of
South America, people are hungry. How's this for a
terrifying realization: Two-thirds of the people in the
world go to bed hungry every night! They don't have
enough to eat. That realization pierces the heart of
the Savior and those who follow him. He reminds us
that when we answer the need of the hungry, we are
really answering his need. Check that last sentence
against Matt. 25:31-46. I think Jesus really cares about
feeding folks. What do you think? More important,
what will you do?

 Lord, make me attentive to the eating habits
of others, especially those who would like to get
into the habit of eating regularly, but can't.
Amen.

**Write to CARE or Bread for the World. Ask how you
can help. Send a dollar in your letter.**

■ SUFFERING AND COMPASSION

Luke 10:29-37: " . . . and when he saw him,
he had compassion on him . . . " (v. 33 KJV).

How's your suffering style? Do you moan and groan
a lot when you're in pain? Or are you a stiff-upper-
lipper? Most of us don't really know too much about
our suffering style because we don't suffer much.
Thank God for that! But turn the suffering coin over.
Look at the other side: compassion. How's your
compassion style?

Most young people are very compassionate when
personally confronted with another's pain. Kids really
help out, and help out quickly. That's great! But
when the ache in the world is a bit more abstract, the
compassion wanes. I mean, how's your compassion
toward all those "invisible" old people tucked behind
the walls of nursing homes? How's your compassion
toward the kids who never complain but struggle
away in school trying to help their single-parent
families keep things together? How's your compassion
toward the people in the ghetto whose first task each
morning is figuring out how to find some food?

Jesus was compassionate. He heard and helped. He
had compassion for the hungry crowds. He had
compassion for a weeping widow. He had compassion
for 10 lepers. His heart went out to need. He has
compassion for you.

Melt my slightly frozen heart, Lord, with the
warmth of your caring. Help me hear the cries of
need and offer my compassionate response.
Amen.

**Look around your community. What calls for
compassionate attention? Organize some kids to help.
You can do it!**

■ WHEN YOU'RE AFRAID

John 6:16-21: "Don't be afraid," Jesus told them. "It is I!" (v. 21).

In the early 1930s, Franklin D. Roosevelt delivered a great presidential address featuring the phrase, "The only thing we have to fear is fear itself." Those were reassuring words at a troubled time. They are also largely true. The fear that fear creates is normally much greater than the originating cause.

Fear crops up everywhere in a teenager's life. The toughest fears we deal with are those which are totally imaginary. What shall we do with all our fears?

First, discuss your fears with people who can help you evaluate the accuracy of your judgment. Older friends, maybe?

Second, see if there isn't something you can do to overcome the cause of your fear. Need help studying for a class? How about some instructions on how to dance? A lesson or two on the social graces? Seek out the help you need.

Third, recognize the reality of the presence of God. The disciples on the stormy sea finally turned their attention to the Lord who calmed the troubled waters. As experienced sailors, they went to the limits of their ability and then turned to him for aid. Why don't you do the same thing? Hand in hand with our Lord, every fear is, at the very least, manageable!

Calm me, Lord, and help me see your powerful presence when all I see otherwise is skyscraping fear. Amen.

Make a little list of things you used to fear. Did any of them really hurt you? I mean *really*? How did you overcome them?

■ BE HAPPY! LIVE LONGER!

Phil. 4:4-7: "May you always be joyful in your union with the Lord. I say it again: rejoice!" (v. 4).

According to medical research, happy people live longer, have fewer sicknesses, and have fewer accidents. Sounds good, but how do you become happy?

St. Paul says you just do it. You rejoice. You let bubbling good humor and good-natured acceptance surface within your life. In his letter to the people at Philippi, he urged them a number of times to let joy loose in their lives. The way to do that is by concentrating on the Lord Jesus Christ.

When we concentrate on Jesus, we develop a different view of ourselves. We begin to see *how valuable we are to God.* Just think—God was willing to give his Son to get us back from sin. Now, after life here on earth, we are assured of eternal life with him. That's what makes us happy.

Christians can see themselves as they really are without flinching. We are sinners for sure, but we are *saved* sinners. How about that? Won't that put a grin on your face? Doesn't that fire off Roman candles in your heart? Isn't that additional reason to rejoice?

The scientists say happy people live longer on earth. Better than that, people happy in Christ live forever.

Put the joy, joy, joy, joy down in my heart, Lord. Amen.

Keep track of what makes you unhappy. What do those things have to do with Christ? Think about it.

■ ALL DRESSED UP

Matt. 22:1-14: "The king went in to look at the guests and saw a man who was not wearing wedding clothes" (v. 11).

A person's appearance is very important. Sure, you can say that people who really count can see past the grubby jeans, matted hair, and torn shirt to the real you. But people who care don't force people to look past a consistently unkempt appearance. Sloppiness in dress and appearance is a kind of rude arrognace and a rejection of people. It often masks a hidden fear—a fear people will reject you even if they see you under the best of circumstances.

Of course, you can overdress. You can become selfishly preoccupied with clothes. Just as a dirty and disheveled appearance can be a front behind which you hide, so can clothes of exaggerated style.

The trick is to dress for the occasion in the most sensitive way you can. To a more formal event, wear the best you have. At other events, let your appearance say that you care about your company and desire to make them comfortable.

How can you tell if you err in one way or the other? Easy. Listen to what people say to you, or just ask someone.

The best guide is this: Dress yourself so people will know you view yourself as a child of God.

You gave Adam and Eve proper clothes right away, Lord. Help me to know and appreciate what is proper in my apparel so that I may honor you by my appearance. Amen.

Go through your closet. Do you see the clothes of a Christian? Especially check the printed messages on your T-shirts.

■ DON'T BLAME ME

Luke 14:15-24: "But they all began, one after another, to make excuses. The first one told the servant, 'I have bought a field and I must go and look at it; please accept my apologies" (v. 18).

If you had grown up 30 or 40 years ago, you would be familiar with a character called Alibi Ike. No matter what he did, it wasn't his fault. There was always an excuse—it was always someone else's fault. People like that are a pain.

Of course, there are times when you aren't to blame! But there are usually more times that you are. The ease with which you admit an error marks the level of maturity you have achieved. "Children" are never wrong. Adults are frequently wrong. Often teenagers write to me about the inability of their parents to admit error. I always remind them to check themselves for the same flaw.

The real reason behind making excuses or refusing to admit a mistake is a misunderstanding of forgiveness. People who make mistakes can be forgiven. As a matter of fact, *only* people who make mistakes can be forgiven. The others don't need it. Christ Jesus died on the cross to cover mistakes. That's another way of saying he died to forgive our sins. By accepting his gift and by using him as the model, we can learn to forgive ourselves and others.

 Forgiven people forgive, Lord. I know that. Help me practice what I know. Help me apply forgiveness to myself and to others. I'm tired of making excuses, and getting them too. Amen.

When was the last time you really needed an excuse? I mean *really*! Would "I'm sorry I made that mistake" have worked just as well?

■ MATERIALISM

Exod. 20:17: "Do not desire. . . . "

Wanting what you don't have can ruin your life. In excessive amounts, wanting poisons all other joy of ownership. Yearning for that bigger boat destroys the fun you have on your smaller one. Exaggerated wanting has another name: *materialism.* That word describes a condition in which a person believes that things like gold, buildings, clothing, or cars can bring lasting happiness. They can't; they often simply whet your appetite for larger yearnings.

One way to determine whether you are a materialist is with a simple question: "Do you own your possessions, or do your possessions own you?" A lot of teenagers give up everything—friends, education, everything—just to own a car or a larger stereo. That's dumb. Cars rust. Stereos wear out. Then what do you have?

There's nothing basically wrong with material things in life. A trail bike, your own TV, a canoe, some great clothes—they are all OK. As long as *you own them.* But when they loom over your life so large that everything else shrinks to nothing, then *they own you.* You have become a materialist, and the materialistic miseries will get you for sure.

Listen to Jesus. Read Matt. 6:19-21. Then think about his words.

Let me never forget you are my true treasure, Jesus. Amen.

Go through some advertisements. Circle the things you want. Do you think they will make you happy?
As a check, circle the things you have.
Are you happy with them?

■ WHAT DO YOU VALUE?

Luke 12:13-21: " . . . a person's true life is not made up of the things he owns, no matter how rich he may be" (v. 15).

You have to establish your own values. Others can make suggestions but only you can make the final decision about what is important to you. For example, when home is important, you will make sure you are there at key times like supper or a family weekend. When you give value to education, studying becomes important—even exciting. When a friendship is of value, there will always be time for getting together with your pal.

What are your values in the categories of honesty, dependability, cooperation? Do you have values about sexual morality, stealing, and lying? One way of checking yourself out is by completing a sentence that goes like this: I would never ＿＿＿＿＿＿＿. Or: I would suffer anything rather than ＿＿＿＿＿. Completing these sentences gets your values out in the open!

No matter what you decide, you need to remember that we all still slip, fail, or fall. To put it simply, we sin. God in Christ offers to forgive the real mistakes we make and will cover over our rebellions against him. Ask for forgiveness when you slip and the ability to reclaim your values and try again.

 Give me a high sense of values, Lord. When I fail to act on my understanding, give me forgiveness and help me raise my standards again. Amen.

List two areas where you've let your standards slip. What must you do to reclaim the values you had? Do it.

■ I ACCEPT THE RESPONSIBILITY

Job 19:1-12: "Even if I have done wrong, how does that hurt you?" (v. 4).

Job wasn't happy when he said it, but he did say it. Even though his words came out a little sideways, by his confession Job accepted responsibility for his activities. Confession is not the only way of accepting responsibility though.

You can accept responsibility by stepping forward and taking leadership in a group that has lost its sense of direction. (Could that be your church's youth group, maybe?) You can accept responsibility by deciding to satisfy an overdue need at home. (How about washing and waxing the car, perhaps?) You can accept responsibility by admitting to younger people the difficulties you struggled with and even the failures you experienced while growing up. (Tell your younger brother and his friends the real truth about something you once did.) All those are ways to claim responsibility. Don't drag your feet like Job did. Step right up like the maturing teenager you are and take responsibility.

In a marvelous way, that's exactly what God did for us. He saw our plight and set in motion a great plan for reclaiming all of us. He didn't hesitate to do what had to be done. Our God sent a Savior for us sinners. He accepted responsibility—for you.

 It's great, dear God, that you came to me with what I needed even though you didn't have to. Help me be more responsible in the ministry to others with which you surround me. Amen.

What's the most responsible thing you have ever done? What's the most responsible thing someone else has done for you? Did you thank the one who did it?

■ WE CAN LEARN SOMETHING NEW EVERY DAY

2 Peter 3:18: "But continue to grow in the grace and knowledge of our Lord and Savior. . . ."

You are at the end of this book of devotional Bible readings. Do you realize that you could go right back to the first page and work your way through it again and actually have an entirely new devotional experience? While the Word of God does not change, each of us sure does. God's revelations look different and better at every new angle of age and experience we come upon. It's like climbing a mountain. Each higher vantage point gives a broader and better view of the world. But you've got to climb to know that.

Claim a climbing, growing style. Prepare yourself to improve and mature and learn with every passing day. Look to new experiences as opportunities for a broadening of your perspective and as an extension of your vision. That's what can happen if you don't cramp your growth or restrict your life of Christian service. In every new illustration of God's daily love for you is a larger and better understanding and a brighter view of yourself, your neighbor, and your Lord. Commit yourself to learning by accepting these words of Jesus: "If you obey my teaching, you are really disciples; you will know the truth, and the truth will set you free" (John 8:31-32). You'll be ready to learn something new every day.

 Keep me growing and going, dear Lord, growing in you and going for you. I know I'll learn, and I'll love every minute of it. Amen.

What's the last new thing you learned? Write it down. Replace it every evening with the best new thing you learned during the day.